Passport's Illustrated Travel Guide to

BERLIN

FROM
THOMAS COOK

D0094072

PASSPORT BOOKS
a division of *NTC Publishing Group*
Lincolnwood, Illinois USA

Published by Passport Books,
a division of NTC Publishing Group,
4255 W. Touhy Avenue,
Lincolnwood (Chicago), Illinois
60646–1975 U.S.A.

Written by Chris and Melanie Rice

Original photography by Antony Souter

Edited, designed and produced by AA Publishing.
© The Automobile Association 1995.
Maps © The Automobile Association 1995.

Library of Congress Catalog Card Number: 94-68185

ISBN 0-8442-9076-9

Published by Passport Books in conjunction with AA Publishing and the
Thomas Cook Group Ltd.

Color separation: BTB Colour Reproduction, Whitchurch, Hampshire,
England.

Printed by Edicoes ASA, Oporto, Portugal.

Contents

About this Book

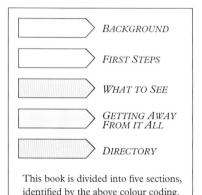

BACKGROUND

FIRST STEPS

WHAT TO SEE

GETTING AWAY
FROM IT ALL

DIRECTORY

This book is divided into five sections,
identified by the above colour coding.

Background gives an introduction to
the city – its history, geography, politics,
culture.

First Steps offers practical advice on
arriving and getting around.
What to See is an alphabetical listing of
places to visit, with walks and tours.
Getting Away From it All highlights
places off the beaten track where it's
possible to relax and enjoy peace and
quiet.
Finally, the ***Directory*** provides
practical information – from shopping
and entertainment to children and
sport, including a section on business
matters.
Special highly illustrated features on
specific aspects of the city appear
throughout the book.

Exhibit of modern art at Berlin's fascinating
Neue Nationalgalerie

BACKGROUND

'It is not at all easy to
visit or live in a city that
is always on
the move, always in the
process of becoming
something else and never
content to stay as it is.'
FRANZ HESSEL

Introduction

*B*erlin is rushing headlong towards the millenium hardly daring to draw breath. The newly designated capital of one of the the largest countries in Europe and of a nation challenged and reinvigorated by unification is also a city with a past at times tragic, at times disturbing, but always fascinating.

Berliners are proud of the sheer size and diversity of their city. Their ancestors in the 19th century looked on in amazement as the boundaries extended ever outward and the population doubled and re-doubled from one generation to the next. Its writers dubbed Berlin a *Grosstadt* (great city) but also a *Weltstadt* (world city) – with connotations of municipal magnificence and civic grandeur, a place where everything is available on a superlative scale and where no one is disappointed. The description is just as applicable to Berlin today.

LOCATOR

It was in the 19th century, too, that Berlin discovered its reverence for the civilisations of the past. Modern Berlin still benefits from that superb cultural inheritance in its world-class museums. It's magnificent architectural heritage ranges from the baroque splendour of the Forum Fredericianum to the neo-classical majesty of Schinkel's Schau-spielhaus; from the great palaces built by the Hohenzollerns at Sanssouci and Charlottenburg to the modern architecture of the world-renowned

Bauhaus school. But there is more to Berlin than culture. The neighbourhood of the Kurfürstendamm is a shoppers' paradise: KaDeWe, the largest department store in Europe is itself a tourist sight. No other city in Europe has such an abundance of green spaces. A bus ride away from the Ku'damm is the Grune-wald forest and Wannsee, with its yachting marinas and beaches. To the east is the Müggelsee, quieter nowadays and less commercialised, but no less beautiful.

Above all Berlin is its people – enterprising and energetic, irreverent, with a rich vein of sardonic humour, generous, kind-hearted, tolerant and fun.

Sculpture on Tauentzienstrasse

THOMAS COOK'S
Berlin

Thomas Cook first advertised trips to Berlin in 1880. In 1896 Cooks were appointed Official International Tourist Agents to the Berlin Exhibition offering a first-class return fare to Berlina via Harwich and Hamburg for £3 4s 2d. It remained a popular destination and the first Cooks representative office opened there in 1906 at Weltreiseburo Union.

History

1307

A single administration is formed from the twin communities of Berlin and Cölln.

1417

Frederick of Hohenzollern is proclaimed Elector Frederick I. The Hohenzollern connection with Berlin will last more than 500 years.

1443

Frederick II ('Irontooth') builds the first Berlin *Schloss* or Castle.

1618–48

During the Thirty Years' War Berlin is briefly occupied by Austrian and Swedish forces. The population is halved to about 6,000.

1640–88

Under Frederick William I, the 'Great Elector', the fortunes of Berlin revive. He builds the Stadtschloss at Potsdam as well as a palace and arsenal in Berlin.

1688

Accession of Elector Frederick III. The palace at Charlottenburg is built for Frederick's wife, Sophie Charlotte.

1701

The Elector crowns himself King Frederick I of Prussia.

1713–40

Frederick William I, the 'Soldier King', turns Potsdam into a garrison town and Berlin into a barracks.

1740

Accession of Frederick the Great. Under the influence of the Enlightenment, Berlin is considerably embellished but retains its military character.

1756–63

Seven Years' War. Frederick's expansionist foreign policy leads to the occupation of Berlin by Austrian troops in 1757 and again by Russians in 1760.

1789

Carl Gotthard Langhans designs the Brandenburg Gate as an arch of peace.

1806

Following the defeat of Frederick William III's forces at the battle of Jena, Napoleon enters Berlin and removes the Quadriga (the chariot drawn by four horses) from the Brandenburg Gate. It is restored in 1814.

1810

Humboldt University is founded.

1837

The Industrial Revolution gets underway with the founding of August Borsig's locomotive works in Kreuzberg. Ten years later, Werner Siemens and Johann Georg Halske set up Europe's first plant for manufacturing telegraph equipment.

1848

The social consequences of industrialisation are seen when barricades are set up by rioting crowds. Frederick William IV promises free elections but subsequently goes back on his promise.

1862

William I appoints Bismarck Minister-President of Prussia.

1871

Berlin is proclaimed capital of a newly unified Germany, following France's defeat in the Franco-Prussian War.

1875

Work begins on constructing Berlin's elevated railway, the Stadtbahn.

1888

Kaiser William II becomes ruler of Germany.

1914–18

World War I ends with the abdication of

the Kaiser and the proclamation of a German Republic.

1920
For five days in March, Wolfgang Kapp's right-wing forces control much of Berlin. In the same year eight towns and 59 villages are merged to create Greater Berlin, the population doubling overnight to almost 4 million.

1930
Marlene Dietrich appears in *The Blue Angel*. Inflation and unemployment continue to increase.

1933
Hitler becomes Chancellor of Germany.

1936
Berlin hosts the Olympic Games.

1938
Jewish property is destroyed and synagogues are set ablaze on *Reichskristallnacht* ('the night of breaking glass').

1939–45
World War II.

1945
The fall of Berlin, Hitler's suicide and the capitulation of the German forces. The city is reduced to rubble and the population is driven to cutting down trees in the Tiergarten for fuel. Under Allied occupation, Berlin is divided into four sectors: British, American, Soviet and French.

1948–9
The Soviet Blockade is defeated by the Berlin Airlift, organised by Britain and the US to carry supplies into the city. Germany is divided into the Federal Republic (West) and the German Democratic Republic (East).

1953
Workers' revolt in East Berlin is crushed by Soviet tanks.

1961
The Berlin Wall is built to stem the exodus of East Berliners to the West.

1989
The collapse of Communism in East Berlin and the reopening of the Wall.

1990
The Wall comes down.

1991
The German parliament votes to move the site of the government from Bonn to Berlin by the year 2000.

Frederick the Great encapsulates Prussia's military past

WAR AND PEACE:

For more than 200 years the fortunes of the Brandenburger Tor (Brandenburg Gate) have been inseparably bound up with those of the German people. Designed in 1789 by Carl Gotthard Langhans in neo-classical style, it was intended as a Gateway to Peace. The addition by Schadow of the goddess Viktoria driving her chariot, the Quadriga, four years later when Prussia was at war with France, was designed to reinforce the vision of peace triumphant. When the Prussian army was defeated at Jena, Napoleon entered the city determined to demoralise the vanquished and demonstrate the effectiveness of war. He removed the precious Quadriga and shipped it to Paris as part of the spoils. But the citizens rallied to the flag and Prussia's resistance inspired the entire German people to view her cause as their own. Ultimately they triumphed; Marshal Blücher returned the goddess to the Brandenburg Gate amid scenes of national rejoicing. Langhans' original intentions were quite forgotten in the din, even by the great architect, Karl Friedrich Schinkel, who sought to adorn the wreath of oak leaves decorating Viktoria's staff with the iron cross.

When German unification was finally achieved in 1871, not by democratic means but by 'blood and iron', the celebrations centred on a triumphant procession through the Brandenburg Gate led by the Kaiser and his generals. Who would then have believed that, less than 50 years later, at the end of World War I, the Kaiser's grandson would be driving through the same arch for the last time into exile, bringing to an end more than 500 years of Hohenzollern rule?

In the crisis that followed, Germany was confronted by civil war and revolutionary and government forces in turn took up machine-gun positions on top of the Gate. The darkest era in German history was dawning, when Nazi storm troopers would process under torchlight through the Gate in celebration of a 1,000-year Reich that would be built on hatred, division and war. Instead came defeat and national humiliation: by 1945 Berlin lay in ruins and Soviet troops raised the red flag over the battered, pock-marked arch.

THE BRANDENBURG GATE

Berlin's most enduring symbol –
the Brandenburg Gate

During the Cold War, the Gate became the symbol not of German unity but of her division. Western politicians eagerly seized photo-opportunities to eye the Gate ruefully across no-man's-land, while their eastern counterparts did their best to obscure the view down Unter den Linden by hanging red banners across its columns. When the Wall finally came down in 1989, the Brandenburg Gate took on a new symbolic role – one of hope and renewal. It is a role more in keeping with Langhans' original vision of a gateway dedicated to peace.

Politics

*I*n October 1990 Germany became one nation for the first time in more than 40 years and Berlin became the *de facto* capital of one of the largest countries in Europe. Three months later, the first all-city elections returned a Christian Democratic Union administration, but in view of Berlin's particular problems and in the spirit of compromise, it was decided to appoint a consensus government across party lines.

Seat of government

Soon after the elections, the municipal administration made the symbolic move from the Rathaus Schöneberg, former home of the West Berlin council, to the Rotes Rathaus in the centre of the old city. In June 1991 the Bundestag voted to make Berlin the seat of the German government by the year 2000. The administration will be housed in various parts of the city but the Chamber itself will sit in the old Reichstag building.

In the autumn of 1993 the Defence Ministry became one of the first to move back to Berlin. The choice of offices in the old Bendler Block, where Admiral Tirpitz had masterminded the expansion of the German navy before World War I, was seen by many as insensitive but the minister, Volker Rühe, argued that the role played by the building in the Von Stauffenberg plot against Hitler, in July 1944, gave it unimpeachable credentials.

Parliament past and future – the Reichstag building

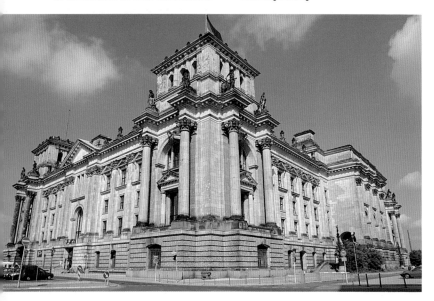

A new mood

While there was genuine pleasure at the news that Berlin was once again to become the capital, the mood has changed noticeably from the euphoria that gripped the people in the heady days of 1989–90. Since then the German economy has gone into deep recession: by the end of 1993 unemployment stood at a record 3.7 million (8 per cent in the West, 15 per cent in the East). East Berliners were experiencing not only economic hardship but a crisis of identity as well. The East German nation, together with the ideology it espoused, had been consigned to the scrapheap: socialism was declared moribund, the currency was pronounced worthless and even national symbols, like the flag, were held up to ridicule. Frustration and disillusionment turned to resentment. West Berliners were perceived as spoilt, arrogant and lacking in ideals. Faced with an erosion in their own living standards, the 'Wessis' (West Berliners) blamed the 'Ossis' (East Berliners) for dragging the economy down. Elements in both communities looked for a scapegoat and found one in their respective immigrant communities – the Turks in the West, the 'guest workers' in the East. The disillusionment became so great that there were even those who, only half jokingly, called for the rebuilding of the Wall, 'only this time five metres higher'.

The future

The issue of racism is particularly sensitive in Berlin, and in other parts of Germany. Clashes between right-wing factions and Turkish immigrants were frequent in the early 1990s. Inevitably anti-Semitism creeps in and there have

Germany is a parliamentary democracy with an electoral system based on constituency voting and proportional representation. The head of the state is the Federal President, elected for five yers by an electoral college comprising representatives of the *Bundestag* and the governments of the 16 *Länder* or states. There is a bicameral parliament comprising the *Bundestag* (House of Representatives) and the *Bundesrat* (Federal Council). There are five major parties: the Christian Democratic Union (CDU), the Christian Social Union (CSU), the Social Democratic Party (SDP), the Free Democratic Party (FDP) and the Greens.

been a number of attacks on Jewish monuments and memorials. A sense of perspective is needed when looking at Berlin's problems. The worries that preoccupy Berliners are much the same as those affecting the citizens of Europe as a whole. Looked at more objectively, despite all the problems that Berlin faces, the long term future for the city looks bright. The levels of investment are unprecedented, as any visitor can see in the number and scale of building developments currently going on all over the city. Berlin has a level of subsidy which many cities can only dream of, a geographical position right at the heart of Europe and unprecedented opportunities for tourism. And no matter what Berliners have to say about one another, East and West, they have an equal capacity for hard work and a heartfelt desire to see their city succeed.

Geography

*B*erlin lies on a vast lowland plain in northeastern Germany, which accounts for the almost total absence of hills – nowhere is higher than about 70m above sea level. The city was founded at the lowest crossing point of the Spree. The sandy terrain, punctuated by rivulets, bogs and channels, continues to affect the foundations of buildings to this day. But the soil also accounts for the proliferation of woodland which, despite having been cleared repeatedly over the centuries, continues as a source of relaxation and enjoyment for Berliners. Today there are about 3.5 million Berliners, and the city is still Germany's largest, extending over an area of about 1,000sq km, more than one-third of which consists of forests, fields and lakes.

Climate

Officially Berlin has a continental climate, but the cold winters one would expect at this latitude, brought in by the Siberian blast from the east, are modified by warmer fronts emanating from Western Europe. Summers can be fresh and sunny, but are not usually very hot. Rainfall is substantial but is distributed fairly evenly throughout the year.

Nightfall over Bismarckstrasse

Economy

Berlin's industrial base is concentrated in the eastern half of the city where food processing and consumer industries exist alongside large-scale engineering plants. The economy in the west still suffers from a long-standing dependence on massive American and later West German investment, a consequence of its peculiar geographical and political isolation. Since reunification the situation in Berlin mirrors the rest of the country, the main problem being how to integrate two such disparate economies. Industry in the East still suffers from outmoded technology and low productivity and is struggling to compete. High unemployment is another unwelcome outcome of exposure to the chill winds of market capitalism. The policy of the united German government, put crudely, is to subsidise the East with grants, low interest loans and tax incentives – a fearfully expensive solution which is already facing stiff opposition from many quarters.

Pollution

Berlin's reputation for invigorating air, the famous *Berliner Luft*, is being

Open spaces are to be found everywhere in Berlin – the Tiergarten

challenged by pollution. The sources are easily identifiable – factories producing sulphur dioxide and car and bus emissions of nitrogen oxide. Some of the culprits have been exposed and are currently being taken to task.

Cleaning up is now a priority. Recycling of all waste products, long practised in the West, is now being encouraged in the East. Restrictions are being introduced on the use of brown coal as a source of energy. Car-owners are being urged to buy lead-free petrol and to use the city's first-rate public transport system whenever possible. In connection with this there is a campaign to make the Ku'damm car-free. But because the GDR had no environmental policy, it could be a while before a clean-up is complete.

ICH BIN EIN BERLINER

Berliners and tourists come together on Kurfürstendamm (Ku'damm)

It is characteristic of Berliners that even in the most trying circumstances they retain their sense of humour. So it was to be expected that when President Kennedy came to the city in 1963 to show solidarity with the beleaguered inhabitants and proclaimed '*Ich bin ein Berliner*' ('I am a Berliner') there were more than a few wry smiles among his audience – a 'berliner' is also a kind of doughnut.

Berliners are, as they always have been, quick-witted, energetic, industrious, sentimental, generous, ebullient, sophisticated and arrogant. It is this last trait that is the origin of the

President Kennedy is still remembered in Berlin

manager what it meant to be a Berliner was introduced to the staff – an Italian, a Lebanese, a Yugoslav and an Egyptian.

And what of the 'Ossis' and 'Wessis', inhabitants of a long-divided Berlin now thrown together like a shy couple at a rowdy dance? Understanding between the two communities is not always easy, but the resilience, the courage and above all the humour typical of Berliners remains common to both. It was, after all, an East Berliner who apologised on behalf of Marx and Engels: 'Sorry but it's not our fault. Maybe next time things will turn out better.'

term *Berliner Schnauze* or 'mouth', implying a tendency to shout people down, to feel superior, to be a bit of a 'know-all'. Two hundred years ago the poet Goethe put it more circumspectly: the Berliner, he suggested was 'somewhat forward'. But the Berliners themselves talk of *Herz und Schnauze* ('heart and mouth') – they are, they will assure you (and it is difficult not to agree with them) big-hearted and thoroughly likeable.

Berlin, more than ever nowadays, is a cosmopolitan city. A significant proportion of the guest workers who began to arrive from Turkey, Yugoslavia and the Middle East in the '60s and '70s have set up home here, adding extra breadth and a little spice to the Berlin persona. There is the story of a visitor to a restaurant, who having asked the

Rocking in the Europa Center

Culture

Berlin takes its culture seriously, but no two Berliners can agree on what that culture is. The result is an almost anarchic diversity, spawning an unusually rich diet. Cultures, mainstream and alternative, compete on every level but in an atmosphere of friendly rivalry.

To explore Berlin is to experience this range of cultures. Begin at the Ku'damm where you'll find the international culture that is available in every European city – Hollywood blockbusters, musicals and discotheques. Even

cabaret, once notorious for its biting satire and subversive irony has succumbed to the new internationalism.

For hardhitting politcal satire or '20s nostalgia, you'll have to look further, to the clubs around Friedrichstrasse, where nightlife was born at the turn of the century. Culturally, Berlin has always embraced the notion of sexual liberation. Nollendorfplatz is still as much the focal point for the gay and lesbian community as it was 60 years ago.

Berlin's high culture is more geographically dispersed. The city's peculiar status during the Cold War allowed it, almost in spite of itself, to play off the rival ideological camps to advantage. The result, as Berliners never tire of boasting to visitors, is at least two of everything (there are three opera houses).

Kreuzberg and Prenzlauer Berg are citadels of the alternative culture, spawning here-today, gone-tomorrow art galleries, events and happenings, exhibitions and impromptu performances of all kinds. Kreuzberg is also known as 'little Istanbul' because of its large Turkish community – the streets between Hallesches Tor and Schlesisches Tor have a distinct flavour of the orient, with bazaars and exotic restaurants.

Culture is not what it was in Berlin – and therein lies the secret of its success. For while other cities look back with nostalgia to their artistic and cultural heritage, Berliners look forward to the future; which is why the city is set to win a place in the cultural heart of Europe.

The old Arsenal (Zeughaus) now houses the Museum of German History

Ir				Std.	Tag
esden ★	incl. Mittagessen / lunch			10	Di/Do Tu
reewald ★	only b				1.5. – 2.10.
tsdam ★	incl. S				
rlin City					
reewald ★	incl. Ka				
rlin City	Berlin Vision			1,5	täglich/d
rlin City East				3,5	täglich/d
	incl. Schiffsfahrt / boat trip				9.4. – 31.1
per Berlin	incl. Haus am Checkpoint Charly			3	täglich/d
rlin City	Berlin Vision			1,5	täglich/d
rlin City	Berlin Vision			1,5	täglich/d
rlin City	Berlin Vision			1,5	täglich/da
reewald ★	incl. Kahnfahrt /punting trip			7	Mi/Wed 2.
us-/Schiffs (boat) Tour				4,5	täglich /d
	incl. Neuer Garten in Potsdam				
ensteine der Geschichte / historical tour					
rlin City	Berlin Vision			15	täglich /d
tsdam ★	incl. Schloßbes				ich /da
per Berlin	incl. Perg				ich /d
Big Berlin - Fo					ich /da
	mit 5 Stops				
rlin City	Berlin				ich /d
rlin City	Berlin				ich /da
ghtclubtour ★	mit / with dinner			4,5	Sa /Sat
ghtclubtour ★	ohne / without dinner			3,5	Sa /Sat

FIRST STEPS

'Its liberal, tolerant
tradition, its contradictions,
the sardonic humour
of its people, and the sense
of a living past that
it has learned to integrate...'

WIM WENDERS
film director, on the appeal of Berlin

First Steps

*B*erlin has been more generously endowed than any other city in Europe of its size with lakes, forests and rivers, as anyone flying over the metropolis on a clear day will immediately appreciate. No wonder that even Berliners used to the hectic pace of life here drop everything and 'head for the hills'. The natural beauty of the surroundings makes up for the disorderly character of the city itself, partly the legacy of wartime destruction, partly the result of the Berliner's obsession with rebuilding ever bigger and better.

Arriving

All three Berlin airports are surprisingly close to the city. Most international flights from Western Europe and the US pass through Tegel, which is about 8km to the north and can be reached by bus or taxi. Schönefeld, in former East Berlin, is favoured by many charter companies and is accessible by S-Bahn. The former military airport at Tempelhof is only about 15 minutes from downtown Berlin by U-Bahn (Platz der Luftbrücke station, not Tempelhof).

Many of Berlin's major rail terminals were destroyed during World War II and never rebuilt. The existing termini, Hauptbahnhof and Bahnhof Lichtenberg, are not convenient but are part of the S-bahn circuit. Bahnhof Zoo is in the centre of town, near the Ku'damm.

Getting your bearings

The Wall is a thing of the past but Berlin is still in many respects two cities, divided by the great park called the Tiergarten. Berlin's most famous street, the Kurfürstendamm (known locally as the Ku'damm) is in the West. It is, first and foremost, a shopping street, although there are theatres, cinemas, restaurants and nightclubs here too. Many of Berlin's largest and best hotels are also in the Charlottenburg district.

Many stations are architectural monuments: Wittenbergplatz U-Bahn

An open-top bus is the ideal way to get around and see the sights

The historic heart of Berlin is in the East, starting with the Brandenburg Gate, which presides over one end of Unter den Linden. This majestic avenue was once the main thoroughfare of Imperial Berlin and shops and cafés are beginning to appear again, although nightlife comes to a stop much earlier here than in the West. Former East Berlin contains most of the city's historic buildings and monuments, as well as Museumsinsel (Museum Island). Berlin's horrendous but unmistakable television tower, the Fernsehturm, is also in the East. More than 300m high, it offers a panorama of the entire city. An alternative viewing point in the West is the Europa-Center.

Central Berlin was devastated by Allied bombing during World War II and this still presents orientation problems. At night, especially, the area bordering Potsdamer Platz, Leipziger Strasse and Wilhelmstrasse more closely resembles the fringes of a city than its heart. There is virtually no life here, but the area has been scheduled for re-development.

Where to next? Visitors on the Ku'damm getting their bearings

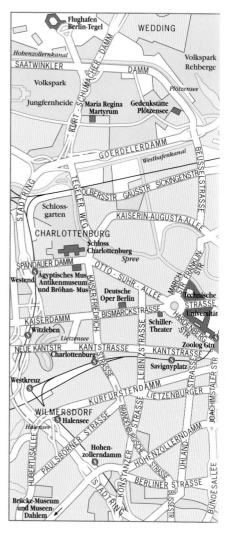

Road system

Berlin is already fully integrated into the German road system. A ringroad surrounds the city with access from north and south. There are major routes out of Berlin to Rostock and Hamburg in the north; Hannover and Braunschweig in the west; Nürnberg (Nuremberg) and München (Munich) in the south and Frankfurt an-der-Oder and Szczecin (Poland) in the east. Having arrived in Berlin, leave the car in a long-stay car park. The public transport system is efficient and not overly expensive, while driving can be a nightmare. Road surfaces, especially in the East, are uneven and poorly lit and there are trams to negotiate. The one-way system presents problems of its own, such as long stretches of road with no left turn.

Getting around

Berlin is a very large city, and the discouragingly long streets induce fatigue all too easily. The best advice is to restrict walking to a stroll through the

BERLIN

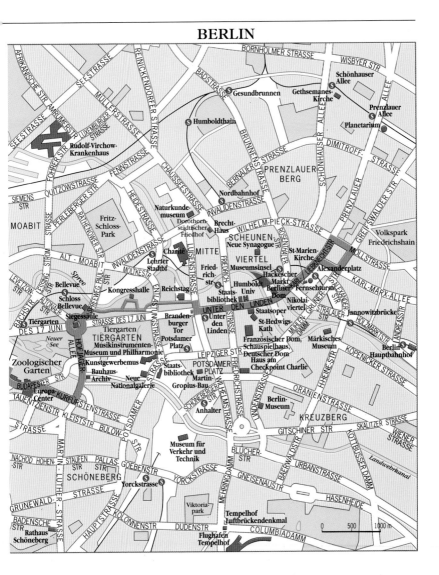

Tiergarten or the Grunewald Forest. Incidentally, when walking beware of straying on to cycle lanes (marked in red). Cyclists travel along these lanes at great speed and with little regard for wayward pedestrians.

Maps and streets

An up-to-date map is a priority, and here the stress should be on up-to-date. As with other cities in the former Eastern Bloc there has been an orgy of name-changing: at the last count more than 80 streets were affected, as well as several U- and S-Bahn stations (Marx-Engels Platz, for example, has reverted to Hackescher Markt). Generally speaking the process is complete but there are likely to be some isolated changes in the future (there are plans to name a street after the former Chancellor and Mayor of West Berlin, Willi Brandt, for example – Wilhelmstrasse has been mentioned as a possibility). Bear in mind, too, that in some of the outlying suburbs the old street signs remain in place. That being said, the most reliable map is produced by the German automobile association – the Berlin ADAC Stadtplan, which includes plans of the Mitte and Tiergarten as well as the new postal codes.

Transport

Few cities in Europe have such a comprehensive public transport system as Berlin. Single journeys are relatively expensive, so before you do anything else buy a travel card from Zoo Station, or from the BVG-Pavillon opposite on Hardenbergplatz, where maps and timetables are also on sale. The 24-hour ticket (24-Stunden-Karten) and the weekly Umweltkarte allow unlimited travel on the entire BVG network (buses, trains, trams and even the ferry from

Trams still run in the former Eastern sector of Berlin

Wannsee to Kladow). Be aware, though, that the weekly ticket runs from Monday to Saturday, so remember to buy a separate day ticket for Sunday. Children under 14 travel at a reduced rate.

There are two complementary urban rail networks: the S-Bahn (Stadtbahn/

Pedestrians beware! Cyclists are to be found everywhere in Berlin

city train), which dates from the 1880s and has long elevated sections punctuated by some striking Jugendstil stations; and the U-Bahn (underground). Both systems are interchangeable but, as a rule, the S-Bahn provides access to the more outlying suburbs such as Wannsee, Oranienburg and Köpenick.

The distinctive cream-coloured double-decker buses round off the transportation network and are also extremely useful for getting about the central areas of the city and the western suburbs. The Ku'damm is made easily manageable by hopping on and off buses, and route 100, which leaves from Zoo Station, provides an excellent service linking the West End with Unter den Linden and Alexanderplatz. (Alight by the stairs at the back.) There is an excellent night-bus service operating throughout the city.

Cycling in central Berlin is feasible provided one knows where one is going. The best places to cycle, however, are the forests and lakes of the outlying suburbs and these can be reached more easily by rail (cycles may be taken onto the S-Bahn – use the doors marked with the relevant symbol).

Language

Generally, language presents few difficulties in Berlin. Berliners do have a distinctive accent but visitors with a knowledge of standard German will encounter few problems. English is in increasingly common use, especially in restaurants, but East Berliners are less likely to speak it as Russian was formerly the first foreign language taught in East German schools.

This way to Berlin's most famous street, commonly called the Ku'damm

The three-card trick is demonstrated on Alexanderplatz

Manners and mores

Much is made of the differences between Berliners and other Germans, and certainly Berliners are more relaxed and easy-going than many of their compatriots. But Berliners are Germans none the less, and share the basic characteristics: respect for order and authority; a passion for cleanliness (though you might not think so wandering around Zoo station), and a certain formality. So say *Guten Tag* before asking for something in a shop and *Auf Wiedersehen* when leaving. If you're trying to weave your way through a crowd say *Entschuldigen Sie* or *Pardon* – which is also what to say if you tread on someone's toes. Jay-walking is frowned on, so don't be surprised if you get disapproving looks for doing so. The Germans also have a deserved reputation for obeying the lights at pedestrian crossings. Berliners are somewhat wayward in this respect but again don't be surprised if someone in the crowd seizes your arm or gives you a short lecture on road safety. Berliners tend to dress informally when dining out but in nightclubs the usual rules – smart but casual – apply.

When to come

With its countless indoor attractions and places of interest, Berlin is a year-round destination. However, if you do come in winter bring plenty of warm clothing: the average temperature hovers around 0°C and it can get much colder. Summers tend to be very changeable – not exceptionally hot and with plenty of rain. But when the sun shines, the forests of Grunewald and the lakes at Wannsee, Müggelsee and elsewhere fill up with hikers, swimmers and tennis enthusiasts. It is here, rather than in the city, that one can still sample the famous *Berliner Luft* or fresh air. Perhaps the best time to visit is the spring and early autumn when sightseeing is less tiring but the out-of-town venues are still practicable. Cinema buffs will want to come in February for the Berlin Film Festival; jazz enthusiasts in July; joggers in October when the marathon takes place.

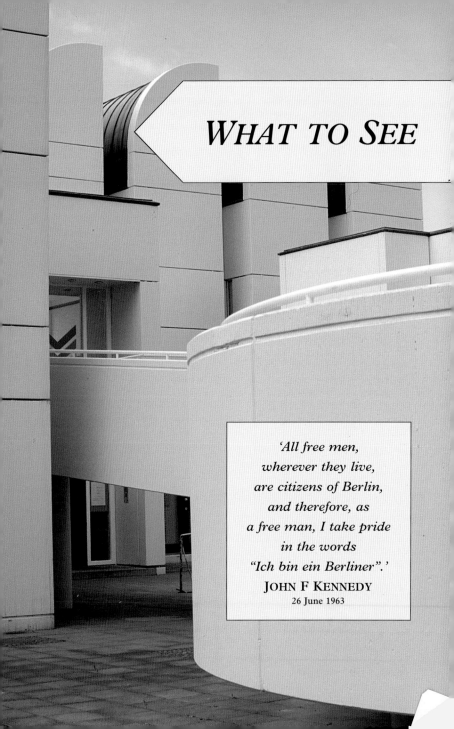

WHAT TO SEE

'All free men,
wherever they live,
are citizens of Berlin,
and therefore, as
a free man, I take pride
in the words
"Ich bin ein Berliner".'
JOHN F KENNEDY
26 June 1963

ALEXANDERPLATZ

'Alex', as the square is affectionately known to Berliners, has had and undoubtedly will see better days. It was originally a wool and cattle market and takes its name from Tsar Alexander I of Russia, who once reviewed the troops here. During the 19th century Alexanderplatz became the centre of working-class Berlin and a focal point of social unrest. The criminal underworld was drawn to the square like a magnet – Franz Biberkopf, the hero of Alfred Döblin's 1928 novel *Berlin Alexanderplatz*, is a convicted murderer who, after his release from prison, sells newspapers on the square. After World War II, Alexanderplatz became a showcase for the 'new' Communist architecture but the end product is predictably sterile: a vast windswept space, intermittently scattered with *imbiss* (snack) stands and market stalls and dominated by the Forum Hotel, whose single virtue is the restaurant on the 37th floor with panoramic views. Perhaps Alex's greatest moment was on 4 November 1989, when half a million East Berliners gathered to protest against the old regime (which collapsed a mere five days later). Sightseeing attractions are thin on the ground; the most noteworthy is Erich John's Weltzeituhr

At the cutting edge of 20th-century design – Bauhaus furniture

THE BAUHAUS

The Bauhaus was founded in Weimar by Walter Gropius, in the climate of frenetic renewal after World War I. Breaking down the artificial divisions between art and architecture, Gropius and his collaborators sought to create a unity of design and an art that was functional rather than decorative, serving the needs of ordinary people. Technology was pressed into service, as well as modern materials like concrete, glass and tubular steel. Awareness of the possibilities of mass production ensured that the Bauhaus's influence would reach far beyond the boundaries of Germany. The Bauhaus was a school of experiment with an unusually free and challenging curriculum. Its teachers were outstanding artistic figures in their own right, some with international reputations: Paul Klee, Vassily Kandinsky, Oskar Schlemmer and Laszlo Moholy-Nagy. There were workshops in furniture, metalwork, print and advertising, photography, wall painting, ceramics, weaving and stage design, loosely co-ordinated by a directorate of Gropius, Hannes Mayer and Mies van der Rohe.

From the outset, the Bauhaus suffered from financial and political constraints. Forced out of Weimar by local right-wing politicians, the school moved to Dessau in 1925 and subsequently to Berlin, where persistent Nazi harrassment finally forced it to close in 1933. Some of the more prominent artists like Gropius and Schlemmer escaped to the US, where their aims and achievements were already well known and from where they continued to exert a major influence. Others, less fortunate, ended their days in concentration camps.

(World Time Clock) in the southern part of the square. Plans are now afoot to regenerate Alexanderplatz with shops and restaurants.
U-Bahn to Alexanderplatz.

BAUHAUS-ARCHIV

This is a fascinating museum of design relating to the history of the Bauhaus (1919–33), one of the most influential artistic movements of the 20th century. The sleek white building with gentle curves in which the exhibition is housed was designed by Walter Gropius in 1964. On display is a representative selection of architectural models and plans, paintings, furniture and domestic objects. Look out for paintings by Klee and Kandinsky, theatre designs by Schlemmer, a silver tea and coffee set by Marianne Brandt (1924), Marcel Breuer's metal-framed chair (1928) and Moholy-Nagy's experimental 'light-space modulator' (1922–30), an extraordinary amalgam of wood, metal, glass and plexiglass which rotates when operated by a button. The overall impression is of having seen many of the items somewhere before, and indeed one has – in the design of countless everyday objects which can be found in late 20th-century homes.
Tiergarten, Klingelhöferstrasse 14. Tel: 2540020. Open: daily except Tuesday, 10am–5pm. Admission charge. Buses 106, 129, 219, 231 to Lützowplatz.

BERLINER DOM (Berlin Cathedral)

Dominating the lower end of Unter den Linden, Berlin's Protestant cathedral was intended as a monument to the Hohenzollern dynasty, more than 90 of whose members lie in the vaults below. A pet project of Kaiser Wilhelm II's, it was designed by Julius Raschdorff in High Renaissance style and opened in 1905 on the site of an earlier cathedral. During World War II it suffered extensive bomb damage and is still undergoing restoration. The dome, which bears more than a passing resemblance to St Peter's in Rome, gives the interior a light and airy feel, in stark contrast to the blackened and rather forbidding exterior. There is an exhibition of historical photographs in the cathedral and occasional organ recitals.

Museumsinsel/Am Lustgarten. Tel: 2469135. Open: Monday to Saturday 9am–5pm, Sunday 11.30am –5pm. Guided tours in English, Thursday 3–5.30pm, Saturday 10.30am–1.30pm. Admission charge. S-Bahn to Hackescher Markt. Buses 100, 157, 348.

BERLIN-MUSEUM

The museum was founded by private initiative shortly after the construction of the Berlin Wall to compensate West Berliners for the fact that the Märkisches Museum was now out of bounds. Nowadays the Berlin-Museum is much the stronger of the two. It presents a satisfying if impressionistic account of everyday life in Berlin from the beginning of the 18th century, using paintings, portraits, maps, models, toys and furniture. The collection is housed in a graceful baroque mansion, designed in 1735 by Philipp Gerlach as the supreme court. A separate exhibition on Jewish history will eventually be mounted in a special annexe.

To the left of the entrance hall are maps, portraits and furniture dating from the 17th and 18th centuries. The most interesting item is the wooden model of the city in 1688, a reminder of the days when Berlin was a stately but modest town with a distinctly provincial feel. Wilhelm Barth's view of the city from bucolic Kreuzberg and Eduard Gärtner's famous panorama of 1832, painted from the roof of Schinkel's Friedrichswerdsche Kirche, both in the upper gallery, confirm that the essential character of Berlin remained unchanged well into the 19th century.

The museum's greatest strength lies in the domestic exhibits. Several rooms on the first floor have been imaginatively furnished and decorated in period styles, from Biedermeier to Jugendstil and are a fascinating testament to changing taste. There are self-portraits by Lovis Corinth, Max Liebermann and Lesser Ury and some expressionistic views of Berlin, for example Ernst Ludwig Kirchner's *Nollendorfplatz*, dating from 1912.

Children will enjoy the toy collection on the top floor – dolls and dolls' houses dating back to the 1830s, a model theatre and grocery shop and a regiment of tin soldiers. The porcelain gallery on the ground floor includes fine examples by the Royal Porcelain Manufacturers (KPM), Chinese vases and figurines and locally produced amphorae.

Before leaving the museum, most visitors call in at the Old Time Weissbierstube, where burgers, pickled herring and white beer are served in period surroundings curiously lacking in atmosphere.

Kreuzberg, Lindenstrasse 14. Tel: 25862839. Open: Tuesday to Sunday

10am–8pm. Admission charge. U-Bahn to Hallesches Tor. Buses 129, 141, 241, 341.

BLOCKHAUS NIKOLSKOE

In 1818 Friedrich Wilhelm III built this wooden cabin in a secluded pine forest as a romantic retreat for his daughter Charlotte and her prospective husband, the future Tsar Nicholas I of Russia (Nikolskoe is Russian for 'belonging to Nicholas'). Perhaps this act of consideration helped cement the marriage, which, by all accounts, was a happy one. Today the Blockhaus is a popular restaurant (crowded in season) with superb views over the Havel. Once you've feasted your eyes, follow the downward slope a short distance to the Church of SS Peter and Paul, which is modelled, like the cabin, on a Russian original. It was built in 1834 by Friedrich Wilhelm Stüler and has a distinctive onion dome.

Wannsee, Nikolskoer Weg. Tel: 8052914. Restaurant open: Friday to Wednesday 9am–10pm; (winter) 10am–8pm. Bus 216 from Wannsee.

Two in one: the Berliner Dom reflected in the Palast der Republic

BERLIN ENVIRONS

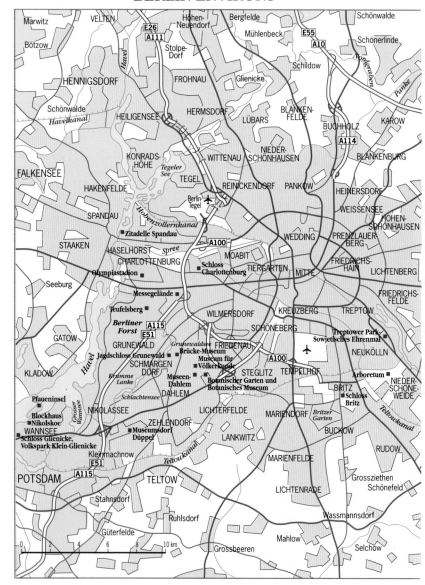

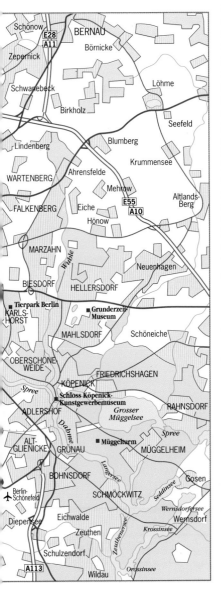

BOTANISCHER GARTEN
(Botanical Garden)

A stroll through the Botanical Garden is the perfect way to relax after visting the Dahlem museums (see pages 46–7). Berlin's first botanical gardens were laid out in the grounds of the royal palace in the 18th century. The move to Dahlem took place in 1899 and the gardens are now home to one of the world's largest botanical collections, with over 18,000 types of plants and flowers. Set in the beautifully landscaped grounds and beech woods are the Jugendstil (art nouveau) glasshouses, housing orchids, palms, ferns, cacti and other exotica against a background of lily ponds and waterfalls. Unless you are a professional botanist, give the adjoining museum a miss and stop off instead at the café near the Unter den Eichen exit.

Steglitz, Königin Luise-Strasse 6–8. Tel: 830060. Open: daily 9am–4pm. Guided tours in English on application two weeks in advance. Admission charge. U-Bahn to Rathaus Steglitz. S-Bahn to Botanischer Garten. Buses 101, 148, 180.

The beautifully landscaped grounds of the Botanical Gardens

BRANDENBURGER TOR
(Brandenburg Gate)

Built on the site of a toll-gate which once marked the western end of the city, the present gate is modelled on the Propylaeum, the entrance to the Acropolis in Athens, and was built between 1788 and 1791 to a design by Carl Gotthard Langhans. The Quadriga surmounting it was added three years later by Johann Gottfried Schadow (see pages 10–11).

Mitte. U-Bahn to Unter den Linden or Bus 100.

BRECHT-HAUS

This house-museum is where the German playwright, Bertolt Brecht (1898–1956), spent the last three years of his life with his actress wife Helene Weigel. First impressions are of austere simplicity and a no-nonsense attitude to a life which revolved wholly around work. The guided tour begins in the small study, an unpretentious room lined with bookshelves stacked to the ceiling with volumes testifying to the erudition

Brecht's eclectic tastes are evident in his library

BERTOLT BRECHT

Brecht achieved overnight fame in 1928 with the Berlin production of *Der Dreigroschenoper* (*The Threepenny Opera*). Kurt Weill wrote the music and his wife, Lotte Lenya, starred as Pirate Jenny. The show was a commercial and literary success but the serious political commitment underlying Brecht's work forced him to leave Nazi Germany in 1933 for America. It was during this exile that he wrote his most influential plays, including *Mother Courage and her Children* and *The Caucasian Chalk Circle*. In 1948 the East German authorities invited him back to Berlin, where he established his own theatre company, the Berliner Ensemble, still in existence today.

A writer's best friend. Brecht's typewriter was in constant use

and eclectic tastes of the man. Standard German classics like Kleist, Schiller, Lessing and Thomas Mann rub shoulders with Shakespeare, Sophocles, Virgil, assorted Chinese and Japanese texts, revolutionary tomes by Lenin and Karl Marx, detective novels and collections of American protest songs. Noh masks and a scroll painting of Confucius are further evidence of Brecht's interest in oriental cultures.

The furnishings are utilitarian, the décor sparse, the floor bare. As Brecht, a committed revolutionary, once told a friend: 'It's a really commendable idea to live in houses with furniture that is at least 120 years old; an early capitalist environment until there is a socialist one.'

The large study, with its view over the garden, was Brecht's favourite working place, each table assigned to a separate

project. Missing from this sanitised museum setting is the sense of creative discovery and the pungent odour of cigar smoke. Late at night Brecht would retire to his bedroom and the newspapers, while downstairs, Helene Weigel created her own, more homely, space. There is a lighter feel here, especially in the conservatory, with its potted plants, Meissen porcelain and domestic bric-à-brac. Both Brecht and Weigel are buried in the adjoining Dorotheenstadt Cemetery (see page 50).

Mitte, Chausseestrasse 125. Tel: 2829916. Open: Tuesday to Friday 10–11.30am, Thursday also 5–6.30pm (except holidays), Saturday 9.30am–1.30pm. Guided tours only. Admission charge. U-Bahn to Zinnowitzer Strasse or Oranienburger Tor.

Bridges

*T*here are more than 15 bridges spanning the Spree in central Berlin alone yet, like the river itself, they are often overlooked. Here are just a handful of the more interesting ones.

GERTRAUDENBRÜCKE

This bridge crosses Fischer-insel close to the point where Berlin and its twin settlement of Cölln were founded. It was built by the Great Elector Frederick William and is named after Gertraud, the patron saint of the poor and of travellers and a favourite with the fishermen who began plying their trade along this stretch of the river in the 13th century. Note the bronze water rats decorating the base of Gertraud's statue.

JUNGFERNBRÜCKE

A little further north of the Gertraudenbrücke, the Jungfernbrücke is the last of what were once nine drawbridges spanning the river. It dates from 1798 and the drawbridge, still intact, rests on a pair of sturdy stone arches. Huguenot girls once sold their silk and lace wares here.

LESSINGBRÜCKE

This elegant iron bridge crosses the bend of the Spree north of the Tiergarten. It is named after one of Germany's best known dramatists, Gotthold Ephraim Lessing (1729–81) and the four piers of red sandstone which complete the design are decorated with a number of scenes from his plays.

MOABITER BRÜCKE

The next bridge along from the Lessingbrücke, on Bellevue Ufer, the Moabiter Brücke was built in 1894 and blends in well with the background of industrial warehouses. Its most prominent features are the streetlamps which serve to decorate the parapet, and the four bears (the bear being the symbol of Berlin).

MOLTKE BRÜCKE

One of the most impressive of Berlin's bridges, the Moltke Brücke stands on Kronprinzen-Ufer, between the Kongresshalle and the Reichstag. It is named after Field Marshal Count Helmuth von Moltke, hero of the three wars which brought about German Unification – against Denmark in 1864, Austria in 1866 and France in 1870. Predictably, the mood of the bridge is triumphant – splendidly bellicose Prussian eagles stand guard over the trophies of war while martially clad cherubs sporting swords, as well as drums and trumpets, decorate the base of the iron lamposts. Completed in 1891, the bridge was destroyed during World War II and re-erected in 1986.

MONBIJOU BRÜCKE

The name of this bridge commemorates a royal palace, designed by Knobelsdorff as a residence for Frederick William III's widow in 1740. The palace occupied the site of the nearby park but was destroyed in 1945 and never rebuilt. The plain stone bridge is otherwise unremarkable, except that it offers fine views of the Bode-Museum (see page 74), arguably the most handsome of the buildings on Museum Island.

The views are impressive from the Schlossbrücke (Palace Bridge)

SCHLOSSBRÜCKE

Far and away Berlin's best known bridge, and justifiably so, the Schlossbrücke (Palace Bridge) was designed by Karl Friedrich Schinkel in 1819 to replace the decaying Hundebrücke (Dog's Bridge). It stood between the former Schloss and the Lustgarten and still offers a commanding view of Schlüter's masterpiece, the Zeughaus, as well as the unmistakable Berliner Dom. The outstanding feature of the bridge, an admirable blend of iron and stone and a splendid engineering achievement, is the marble statues of Greek gods, executed a little later by pupils of Rauch, but to designs by Schinkel. These induced 19th-century Berliners, with a typically mischievous show of humour, to rechristen the bridge the Dolls' Bridge (Puppenbrücke). Less humorously, the Communists named it in honour of Marx and Engels, but it has now reverted to its original name.

BRITZER GARTEN

Situated deep in the southern suburbs, between Mariendorf and Buckow, the Britzer Garden occupies the 100-hectare site of the 1985 National Garden Show, the brilliant creation of the landscape designer, Wolfgang Miller. The visitor is greeted by an artificial but convincing vista of gently undulating hills, lakes and meadows. However, before entering the garden, it is worth leaving the bus at the junction of Britzer Damm and Tempelhofer Weg to have a look at the 13th-century church, with its village pond and 18th-century castle, the Schloss Britz. The gardens are a favourite with Berliners walking their dogs as well as with cyclists and water sports enthusiasts. In the summer there are lively open air concerts by the lakeside, with music catering for every taste. Children's entertainers are also out in force, the puppet shows being a perennial favourite. There are plenty of places to eat, including the Café am See on the northern side of the lake and the restored miller's house (near the old windmill), which has been converted into a rather pricey restaurant.

Neukölln, Sangerhauser Weg 1. Tel: 700–9060. Buses 144, 179, 181.

BRÜCKE-MUSEUM

An unlikely but delightful location for a museum, beside a lake on the fringes of the Grunewald forest. This is an essential port of call for anyone wishing to understand the development of modern art in the 20th century. Die Brücke (the bridge) was a group formed in Dresden in 1905 by Ludwig Kirchner, Fritz Bleyl, Erich Heckel and Karl Schmidt-Rottluff,

Statue of Heinrich Zille and friend at the Märkisches Museum

self-taught artists with a keen interest in experiment. The result was the first wave of German Expressionism, a movement devoted to exploring man's inner landscape rather than objective reality, and characterised by bold use of colour and seemingly uncontrolled brush strokes. Die Brücke, which later included Emil Nolde, Max Pechstein and Otto Mueller, was clearly influenced by Gauguin, Van Gogh and, most importantly, Cézanne, who also had a major impact on the Cubists. The group moved to Berlin for commercial reasons in 1911 and flirted briefly with the artistic ideas of the New Secession; it broke up in 1913.

The museum owes its existence to the longest surviving member of the group, Schmidt-Rottluff, who donated 74 of his own paintings on his 80th birthday in

Conducive to quiet reflection – the Brücke-Museum of modern art

HEINRICH ZILLE (1858–1929)

A prolific artist and popular illustrator, Zille both amused and educated successive generations of Berliners with his witty, sometimes sentimental, but always provocative depictions of the daily lives of workers, the *demi-monde* and the criminal classes – a world which became known as Zille's Milljöh (milieu). For years, Zille was a regular contributor to satirical journals like *Die lustigen Blätter* and *Simplizissimus*. Today his drawings are highly prized collectors items but examples of his work can be found in the Zille-Museum (see page 71) and the Berlin-Museum (see page 30). There is a statue of him outside the Märkisches Museum (see page 68) but his favourite habitat was the old pub, Zum Nussbaum, in the Nikolai Quarter.

1964. By the time the building was completed in 1967 considerable progress had been made in locating and purchasing the works of other artists from private collectors, a task made all the more valuable by the fact that many of the paintings had been destroyed in the Nazi era. The museum is small – just three exhibition rooms – and conducive to quiet reflection. One drawback: only one of the artists is generally exhibited at any one time. Paintings to look out for include Kirchner's *Berlin Street Scene* (1913), Erich Heckel's *Young Man with Girl* (1905), Max Pechstein's *Fishing Boat* (1913) and Schmidt-Rottluff's portrait of Rosa Schapire (1911). *Zehlendorf, Bussardsteig 9. Tel: 8312029. Open: daily except Tuesday, 11am–5pm. Admission charge. Bus 115 to Pücklerstrasse.*

Charlottenburg Museums

*A*ll the following museums are either close to or part of Schloss Charlottenburg (see pages 86–7). It is possible to buy a single ticket to cover all the museums but a tour of the Schloss must be paid for separately.

ÄGYPTISCHES MUSEUM
(Egyptian Museum)

There are plans to reunite this collection with its other half, separated during World War II and currently housed in the Bode-Museum; until then the Charlottenburg branch offers the choice exhibits. Berlin's celebrated romance with Ancient Egypt began in 1698 but it was only in the early 19th century that the romance blossomed into a full-blown love affair. This was largely due to one man, Carl Richard Lepsius, who spent eight years in Egypt in the 1840s before returning with the biggest haul of Egyptian antiquities the world had ever seen. The Charlottenburg display is a joy from start to finish – beautifully presented, manageable and of superb quality.

The star exhibit in the main hall is the exquisite head of Queen Nefertiti, aunt of Tutankhamen. It was discovered in 1912 by the Berlin archaeologist Ludwig Borchardt among the plaster casts of an ancient sculpture workshop dating back to around 1340BC. The incomplete state of the left eye indicates that this head, too, was intended to be a model. This stunningly beautiful queen

Serene Queen Nefertiti, a long-time Berlin favourite

wears a tall blue crown wound with a band of gold and semi-precious stones. The sacred serpent or Uraeus, symbol of royalty, is coiled above the forehead. The surviving eye is made from a shell of rock crystal, into which a black-paste iris has been set. Nefertiti's beauty may be unrivalled but it is Queen Hatshepsut who has the distinction of being the only woman ever to rule Egypt as pharaoh. The mottled granite bust of this unique ruler represents her as an honorary man, complete with ceremonial beard. Another striking exhibit is the so-called Berlin Green Head, dating from the Ptolemaic period (about 300BC). The forceful intelligence of the subject, a priest, is superbly captured by the sculptor, who includes such fine detail as the crow's feet around the man's eyes.

Elsewhere in the museum are bronzes, painted sarcophagi, papyri, jewellery, mummies, death masks, clothing, vials of perfume, vases, gaming boards and musical instruments dating from 5000BC to AD300.

In the entrance to the former livery stables stands the 2,000-year-old Kalabasha Gate, a gift from the Egyptian government. Constructed under the Ptolemies, it was later decorated with reliefs of the

Emperor Augustus, posing rather improbably as Pharaoh. *Charlottenburg, Schlossstrasse 70. Tel: 320911. Open: Monday to Thursday 9am–5pm, Saturday and Sunday 10am–5pm. U-Bahn to Richard-Wagner-Platz. Buses 109, 110, 145.*

ANTIKENMUSEUM (Museum of Antiquities)

Like the Egyptian museum across the road, this neo-classical

Berlin is a treasure-house of Egyptian antiquities

building is the work of F A Stüler and was erected in 1859 as the barracks of the Garde du Corps. The museum contains about half the contents of the former Antiquarium, one of the classical departments of the Prussian state museum, unfortunately dispersed in the chaotic aftermath of World War II. There are plans afoot to reunite this collection with its equivalent in the Pergamon Museum (see pages 76–7). In the meantime the Antiken offers a

fabulous representation of decorative art from the ancient world. On the ground floor, look out for the Corinthian helmet, which evokes the great confrontations between the Greeks and the Persians; also the idol from the Cycladic Islands, strikingly modern in appearance. Highlights on the first floor include the exquisitely proportioned 'amphora of the Berlin painter', a bust of Cleopatra and a playful sculpture of a boy removing a thorn from his foot. The Treasury, on the second floor, displays a hoard of Roman silver discovered at Hildesheim in 1868.

Schlossstrasse 1. Tel: 320911. Open: Monday to Thursday 9am–5pm, Saturday and Sunday 10am–5pm.

Ancient frieze in the Antikenmuseum

The Galerie der Romantik occupies the eastern wing of Schloss Charlottenburg

BRÖHAN-MUSEUM

Based on the private collection of
Professor Karl Bröhan who presented it
to the people of Berlin in 1983, this
unusual museum consists of art nouveau,
Jugendstil and art deco furniture, glass,
ceramics, silver and industrial design
from the turn of the century to the
1930s. New techniques of burnishing
and glazing, developed in the 1870s,
revolutionised ceramics and glass design
throughout Europe and the US. In
Berlin a leading role was played by the
chemical research institute attached to
the Royal Porcelain Manufacturers
(KPM) under Hermann Seger, examples
of whose work can be seen in room 18.
Equally striking are the metal-mounted
pieces of Bohemian glass in the Salon
Hector Guimard, one of a number of
rooms decorated with period contents
and named after a leading manufacturer
or designer. There are some fine early

20th-century paintings and drawings,
too, notably works by Willy Jaeckel, Karl
Hagemeister, Hans Balushchek and Jean
Lambert-Rucki.
*Schlossstrasse 1a. Tel: 3214029. Open:
Tuesday to Sunday 10am–6pm, Thursday
to 8pm.*

GALERIE DER ROMANTIK
(Gallery of the Romantics)

Currently occupying the eastern wing
of the Schloss, the collection, part of
the National Gallery of Berlin, will
eventually be housed in an extension
of the Neue Nationalgalerie in the
Tiergarten. Choice works of the German
Romantic school are presented in the
gallery. Pride of place belongs to Caspar
David Friedrich (1774–1840), whose
work epitomises the Romantic
preoccupation with man's relationship to
nature. One of the finest examples is
Monk at Sea (1808–10) which breaks all

the rules of traditional landscape painting to striking effect. Karl Friedrich Schinkel (1781–1841) made his reputation as an architect, but his talents were by no means confined to building. Schinkel's interest in the medieval world, a typically Romantic passion, is perfectly illustrated by a series of paintings of imaginary Gothic cathedrals set against dramatic natural back-drops. His imagination was equally fired by the classical world, as one can see in *Antique City on a Mountain*, dating from about 1805. Here formal architectural beauty combines sensuously with human activity and the soft majesty of nature. Less elevated, but of considerable historical interest, are the topographical paintings by Eduard Gärtner, including a mid-19th-century view of Unter den Linden and a study of the Bauakademie, one of Schinkel's finest architectural achievements, bulldozed by the East German authorities in the 1960s. The nearby Schinkel Pavilion, an adjunct to the Gallery, has survived as a superb testament to the architect's unsurpassed mastery of form. Displayed in a charming procession of rooms are more paintings from the Romantic period, including a remarkable panorama of the Berlin skyline by Gärtner, from the vantage point of Friedrichswerdersche Kirche.
In the East Wing of the Schloss. Tel: 2662650. Open: Tuesday to Friday 9am–5pm, Saturday and Sunday 10am–5pm.

Clara Bianca, Renaissance-style portrait in the Galerie der Romantik

MUSEUM FÜR VOR UND FRÜHGESCHICHTE (Museum of Pre- and Early History)

By no means as dry and dusty as it sounds, the museum began life as a haphazard collection of curios assembled by the Hohenzollerns. The tribal history of the Germanic peoples is illustrated with a fascinating array of artefacts, including Bronze Age weapons and necklaces originating in the Carpathian mountains. Sadly there are only copies of what was once the prize exhibit, Heinrich Schliemann's fabulous Trojan treasure discovered in 1873 and wrongly attributed to King Priam himself. In 1945 the hoard was looted by Soviet troops and spirited away to Moscow, where its existence has only recently been acknowledged. There are plans to loan out the exhibits but the more thorny problem of ownership is yet to be resolved.
In the West Wing of the Schloss. Tel: 320911. Open: Monday to Thursday 9am–5pm, Saturday and Sunday 10am–5pm.

SCHINKEL'S VISION

He was Germany's greatest architect, but he was much more than that: Karl Friedrich Schinkel (1781–1840) was a sculptor, a painter, a set designer, an interior decorator, a towering intellect and a visionary. His legacy to Berlin is cast in stone – his monument, the city itself and particularly its finest avenue, Unter den Linden.

Schinkel was born in Neuruppin in the Mark Brandenburg, the son of a

Protestant pastor. His interest in architecture was fostered by the precocious Friedrich Gilly under whose father he began his training at the Bauakademie (Building Academy) in Berlin. The regulation Grand Tour of Europe followed, firing his imagination, but ultimately leading to frustration – the political turbulence of the Napoleonic period was hardly the climate for ambitious building schemes. Ever the Renaissance man, Schinkel turned instead to painting in a thoroughly Romantic style, inspired partly by the medieval Gothic architecture he had seen on his travels.

A fervent patriot, he volunteered for the Prussian militia and later designed the nation's most revered award, the Iron Cross. In 1816, Schinkel received his first major Berlin

Schinkel's vision of The Golden Age of Greece

Gothic and Classical, Schinkel left his mark on every style

scenery by Schinkel himself, but it was typical of this shy man that when he was called to acknowledge the applause of the audience, he had already sneaked off home.

A flurry of commissions followed: the Altes Museum, the Nikolaikirche in Potsdam, the Friedrichswerdersche Kirche and Schloss Babelsberg. In everything he undertook, Schinkel was conscientious to a fault – no detail was too small for his attention, even a door knob or a lampholder.

But there was a price to pay for all this industry. By the end of the 1830s, Schinkel, one of the world's greatest workaholics, was thoroughly exhausted. He collapsed with a stroke in September 1840 and died without regaining consciousness.

commission, the Neue Wache (Guard House). From this time on, he had to tame his Romantic inclinations in the face of the Hohenzollern royal house's preference for the classical style: undaunted, Schinkel produced a masterpiece. The Schauspielhaus (National Theatre) on Gendarmenmarkt followed. The theatre opened in 1821 with a play by Goethe and

Dahlem Museums

*A*ll the following museums are located in the scenic suburb of Dahlem in a purpose-built complex of buildings, completed in the 1960s. Only one ticket is required for all the collections.

GEMÄLDEGALERIE
(Picture Gallery)

Of the 1,500 paintings housed here, most of them old masters from the 13th to 18th centuries, more than 750 are on display at any one time. The bulk of the collection was acquired in the 19th century and was originally housed in the Altes Museum on Museum Island. After World War II the paintings were dispersed, the lion's share finding its way to the West. There are plans to move at least part of the collection to a new museum building in the Kulturforum, so expect some disruption.

For the time being the ground floor is devoted to medieval and Renaissance German, Dutch and Italian paintings, and French and English art of the 18th century, while the first floor concentrates on paintings of the baroque and rococo periods from France, the Netherlands, Italy and Spain.

Highlights of the German collection include an altarpiece by the Master of the Darmstadt Passion as well as a magnificent sequence of portraits by Dürer and Hans Holbein and some fine work by Lucas Cranach the Elder, notably *Jungbrunnen* (*The Fountain of Youth*). Even more rewarding is the Flemish primitive art, beautifully composed, rich in symbolism and with a

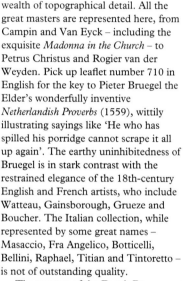

wealth of topographical detail. All the great masters are represented here, from Campin and Van Eyck – including the exquisite *Madonna in the Church* – to Petrus Christus and Rogier van der Weyden. Pick up leaflet number 710 in English for the key to Pieter Bruegel the Elder's wonderfully inventive *Netherlandish Proverbs* (1559), wittily illustrating sayings like 'He who has spilled his porridge cannot scrape it all up again'. The earthy uninhibitedness of Bruegel is in stark contrast with the restrained elegance of the 18th-century English and French artists, who include Watteau, Gainsborough, Grueze and Boucher. The Italian collection, while represented by some great names – Masaccio, Fra Angelico, Botticelli, Bellini, Raphael, Titian and Tintoretto – is not of outstanding quality.

The masters of the Dutch Baroque on the first floor are another matter. Rembrandt's mesmerising self-portrait from 1634 and a study of his beloved wife, Saskia, lead a strong field which includes Frans Hals, Rubens, Vermeer and Van Dyck. The remainder of the collection is a miscellany of baroque and rococo, with representatives from French, Spanish and Italian schools.

All under one roof: the Dahlem Museum complex (right) exhibits art from all periods

KUPFERSTICHKABINETT

This is a small museum of prints, drawings and engravings, much of it of high quality. Among the artists represented are Dürer, Botticelli, Bruegel, Rubens, Rembrandt, Goya; and the moderns Kandinsky, Picasso and Otto Dix.

MUSEUM FÜR INDISCHE KUNST (Museum of Indian Art)

This museum neatly captures the richness and diversity of Indian culture. Artefacts range from prehistoric terracotta and stone sculptures to superb miniature paintings and exquisite examples of craftsmanship in

Arnimallee 23–7 and Lansstrasse 8. Tel: 83011. Open: Tuesday to Friday 9am–5pm, Saturday and Sunday 10am–5pm. U-Bahn to Dahlem-Dorf. Buses 110, 180.

metal, ivory and jade. The art of the Buddhist cave monasteries which once lined the famous Silk Road is also represented.

MUSEUM FÜR ISLAMISCHE KUNST (Museum of Islamic Art)

A remarkable collection of illuminated Korans and manuscripts, glassware, textiles and ceramics covering the entire Islamic world, from Spain to India. The display of Ottoman carpets, mainly dating from the 16th and 17th centuries, is also worth seeing.

MUSEUM FÜR OSTASIATISCHE KUNST (Museum of Far Eastern Art)

One of the best collections in Europe of prints and paintings from China, Japan and Korea, including some superb colour woodblock prints from Japan's Edo period (late 18th century). Other exhibits include a ceremonial axe from China (12th century BC) and finely carved lacquer-ware boxes.

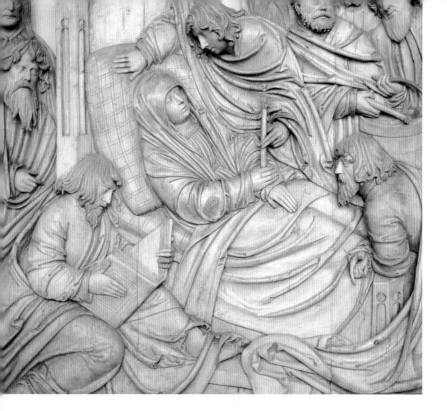

MUSEUM FÜR VÖLKERKUNDE
(Ethnography Museum)

Fifteenth-century carving of the Madonna. One of many on show in the Skulpturengalerie

The Museum of Ethnography was founded in 1873, although its earliest holdings can be traced back to the private collection of the Great Elector in the 17th century. The variety of artefacts from all around the world is so rich and absorbing that it is possible to spend hours here. If time is pressing, try at least not to miss the collection of Oceanian boats, completely reassembled and rigged out as they were in the 18th century. They include a Tongiaki (a kind of catamaran from the island of Tonga) and an ocean-going sailing vessel from the island of Santa Cruz – a marvellous example of the technology of boat-building. There is also a beautifully decorated male clubhouse from the Palau Islands in the Western Pacific.

The museum is divided into eight regional departments. Ancient America includes fine examples of Pre-Columbian gold craftsmanship, Aztec stone figures and the largest collection of Peruvian pottery in Europe. From Africa there are Benin bronzes, carved figures of gods from Cameroon and terracottas from Ife (Nigeria). The Asian display has, among other things, Tang ceramics and, best of all, Indonesian shadow-puppets, masks and theatre puppets. If the visual stimulus is not enough you can hear music from around the world played on original instruments on a bank of headphones near the museum entrance.

SKULPTURENGALERIE

This is a breathtaking collection of sculptures from the late classical period to the 19th century and includes icons and mosaics, medieval religious statuary and some fine examples from the Renaissance and baroque periods.

The sculpture gallery originated with the Great Elector (1640–88) but it was not until 1885 that Wilhelm von Bode, director of the Altes Museum, found it necessary to establish a separate 'Department of Sculptural Works belonging to the Christian Epoch'. The present museum, containing some 1,200 works of sculpture, is divided into five sections: Early Christian and Byzantine; medieval sculpture; the Italian collection; Renaissance and baroque sculpture from north of the Alps; and sculpture of the 19th century. The Renaissance serves as an approximate dividing line between the ground and first floors of the gallery.

The Byzantine era is represented by icons, mosaics and ivories, including a diptych of Christ and the Mother of God dating from the middle of the 6th century. The medieval collection is astonishingly rich, given the iconoclasm which led to the destruction of so many religious objects during the Reformation in Europe.

Among the earliest examples is a dignified figure of Mary, mourning the loss of her son (c1230). Also look out for a serene Christ and St John, from Lake Constance (c1320) and another graceful carving of Mary, from Lindenholz (1480), which depicts the Mother of God as a golden-robed beauty protecting a group of medieval worshippers in the folds of her blue mantle. The Palm Sunday Christ on a Donkey from Landshut would originally have been pulled along in the Holy Week procession – hence the platform on wheels. The donkey and platform are modern replacements but the figure of Christ is original (c1200). Especially absorbing is the Calvary commissioned in about 1490 by the famous Augsburg banking family of Fugger. Among over 30 figures gathered at the scene of the crucifixion are gold-armoured soldiers on horseback, jeering bystanders and the desolate figure of Veronica with a towel to wipe the face of Christ.

The upper floor begins with a room devoted to the work of Tilman Riemenschneider and includes his wonderfully wrought carvings of the four evangelists, each individually characterised. The Italian collection includes a marble relief by Donatello, and sculptures by Bernini and Giovanni Bologna.

Exquisitely painted wooden statue

DEUTSCHER DOM
(German Cathedral)

The German Cathedral is situated on the southern side of the Gendarmenmarkt and nicely complements its French twin, the Französischer Dom (French Church) opposite (see page 52). The architect of the elongated domed tower, Karl von Gontard, was described by Frederick the Great as an 'ass' – and this was before the cupola collapsed in 1781. Another architect, Georg Christian Unger, was called in to rectify matters. Nowadays the building is used only for occasional exhibitions.

Mitte, Gendarmenmarkt. Free. U-Bahn to Französische Strasse.

DOROTHEENSTÄDTISCHER FRIEDHOF (Cemetery)

Founded in 1762 for the deceased of Dorotheenstadt, one of several new suburbs growing up around the old city, the cemetery is an appropriately ethereal setting for the graves of distinguished Berliners, including the playwright Bertolt Brecht and his wife Helene Weigel, the architect Karl Friedrich Schinkel, and the philosophers Hegel and Fichte, university colleagues as close to one another in death as they were in life. One of the more elaborate monuments, featuring sculpted children beneath a classical portico, is the tomb of the railway industrialist, August Borsig. A map beside the cemetery gates will direct you to the celebrities of your choice.

Mitte, Chausseestrasse 126. Free. U-Bahn to Zinnowitzer Strasse.

The three-pointed Mercedes star identifies the Europa Center

EPHRAIM PALAIS

This finely restored rococo mansion with its distinctive golden balconies and sculpted cherubic figures was built in 1766 for the court banker and jeweller to Frederick the Great, Nathan Ephraim. The architect was Friedrich Wilhelm Dietrichs. The original owner's Jewish origins were enough to make the building a target for the Nazis, who wished to widen the adjoining road. The present reconstruction, which preserves Dietrichs' façade, is slightly removed from the original site. On the first floor a museum exhibits maps and paintings from the 17th to the 19th century and is worth visiting just to see the interior of the house. The ground floor restaurant specialises in German cuisine.

Mitte, Poststrasse 16. Tel: 2380900. Open: Tuesday to Friday 9am–5pm, Saturday 9am–6pm, Sunday 10am–5pm. Admission charge. U-Bahn or S-Bahn to Alexanderplatz.

EUROPA-CENTER

This lavish shopping centre, easily identified by the three-pointed Mercedes star on top of the tower block, was opened in 1965 as a showcase for the West German 'economic miracle'. On every visitor's itinerary for its cinemas, theatres, restaurants, casino and night-clubs as well as more than 100 shops, the centre is also notorious among Berliners for its modern sculptures, the most intriguing of which is Bernard Gitton's *Clock of Flowing Time*. There is a tourist information office on the ground floor and a lift will speed you to the top of the building for fine views of the western parts of the city. The site used to belong to the legendary Romanische café, in the '20s the haunt of artists and celebrities ranging from the film idol Elisabeth Bergner to the

The ultimate vantage point – Berlin's 362m Fernsehturm

novelist Thomas Mann and the famous operatic tenor Richard Tauber.

Charlottenburg, Breitscheidplatz. Open: (viewing platform) 9am to shop closing. Admission charge for viewing platform. U-Bahn or S-Bahn to Zoologischer Garten.

FERNSEHTURM

Like it or not, the immense, thrusting television tower, complete with globe and red-and-white striped pole, is one of Berlin's most distinctive landmarks. Rising to 362m, the Fernsehturm is considerably higher than the Eiffel Tower and the views, on a clear day, can be spectacular. There are two vantage points: the viewing platform on the top floor or the Tele-café below.

Mitte, Alexanderplatz. Open: (viewing platform) daily 9am–midnight; closed 9am–1pm on 2nd and 4th Tuesday of each month. Admission charge. U-Bahn or S-Bahn to Alexanderplatz.

Karl von Gontard's distinctive tower crowns the Französischer Dom

FRANZÖSISCHER DOM
(French Cathedral)

On the northern side of the Gendarmen-markt, the French Cathedral was intended for the Huguenot community, invited to Berlin by the Great Elector following the revocation of the Edict of Nantes (1685), which had guaranteed religious tolerance to French Protestants. Its distinctive tower was added between 1780 and 1785 by Karl von Gontard. The small museum of Huguenot history in the base of the tower honours these hardworking people who played a major role in the Prussian manufacturing industry. Climb the spiral staircase to the gallery for fine views of the square and to hear the carillon.

Mitte, Gendarmenmarkt. Tel: 2292042. Open: Museum – Tuesday to Thursday and Saturday noon–5pm; Sunday 1–5pm. Viewing platform open Tuesday to Saturday 10am–4pm. Carillon chimes daily at noon, 3pm and 7pm. Free (admission charge for Huguenot museum). U-Bahn to Französische Strasse.

FRIEDRICHS-WERDERSCHE-KIRCHE (Schinkel Museum)

This finely proportioned red brick church with twin towers was designed by Schinkel between 1824 and 1830 in the late Gothic style which the architect had admired on a visit to England. It was severely damaged during World War II but restored in the 1980s as a museum honouring Schinkel and his contemporaries. There are sculptures in the nave by Schadow, Rauch and Tieck and the wooden gallery chronicles Schinkel's major achievements with plans and photographs of projects like the Schauspielhaus, the original Berliner Dom and the Altes Museum.

Mitte, Werderstrasse. Tel: 2081323.
Open: Wednesday to Sunday 9am–5pm. U-
Bahn to Hausvogteiplatz. Admission
charge.

GEDENKSTÄTTE DEUTSCHER WIDERSTAND (Memorial to German Resistance)

This is where Admiral von Tirpitz planned the expansion of the German navy before World War I and Hitler made his famous *Lebensraum* speech about the German need for 'living space'. In 1944 the building, known then as the Bendlerblock, became the nerve centre for the conspiracy against Hitler led by Chief-of-Staff Count Klaus Schenk von Stauffenberg. When Hitler survived the bomb blast in the command centre at Rastenburg on 20 July 1944, the plot disintegrated. Stauffenberg and three of his colleagues were taken into the courtyard and shot. The other, less fortunate conspirators were taken to Plötzensee prison, where they were tortured then hanged with piano wire, the proceedings being filmed for Hitler's perverted gratification.

A wreath in the courtyard marks the spot where Stauffenberg and his friends were executed, and on the second floor an exhibition charts the history of German resistance. Every oppositionist organisation is credited, from youth groups like the White Rose to trade unionists, Communists and Social Democrats, churchmen and women, Jews and workers. The Bendlerblock has recently been returned to the Defence Ministry amid some controversy.
Tiergarten, Stauffenbergstrasse 13. Tel:
26542213. Open: Monday to Friday
9am–6pm, Saturday and Sunday
9am–1pm. Free. U-Bahn to Kurfürsten-
strasse. Bus 129 to Stauffenbergstrasse.

GEDENKSTÄTTE PLÖTZENSEE (Plötzensee Memorial)

In the grounds of the gloomy prison building, now a remand centre for juveniles, is a paved courtyard with a memorial wall bearing the inscription: 'To the victims of the Hitler dictatorship 1933–1945'. A white urn contains soil samples from each concentration camp. More than 2,500 people died here in the most brutal circumstances. The twin brick buildings behind the wall were the 'death house' and execution chamber. The hooks from which the July plotters against Hitler were hanged have been preserved, the only relics of a nightmarish past. An exhibition of photographs includes death warrants and, even more eerie, the invitation card to an execution. An English leaflet is available on request.
Charlottenburg, Hüttigpfad. Tel: 3443226.
Open: daily March to September, 8am–6pm;
February and October, 8.30am–5.30pm;
January and November, 8.30am–4.30pm;
December, 8.30am–4pm. Bus 123 from S-
Bahnhof Tiergarten. Free.

Monument to victims at Plötzensee

SPY CAPITAL

It was after World War II, when Berlin became in John Le Carré's words, 'the world capital of the Cold War', that the city acquired its reputation for espionage, intrigue and double-dealing. By the early 1950s as many as 12,000 Berliners were earning at least a part-time living from selling secrets to the 'other side'. Money, not ideology, was the main motivating factor: one witness later recalled how 'a few dollars were enough to make many of the boys change sides between cups of coffee'. Defections, kidnappings and mysterious disappearances were an everyday occurrence. It did not matter that the information acquired was generally of a trivial nature. Intrigue is addictive and the rival intelligence organisations – KGB, CIA, SIS, SDECE, Stasi and the rest – lived for the day when they would uncover that elusive military secret. And occasionally they did.

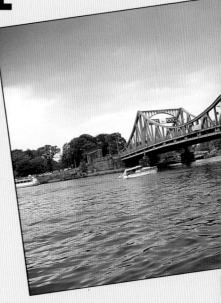

Above: Glienicker Brücke, scene of dramatic spy swaps

Operation Gold (fictionalised recently in Ian McEwan's novel *The Innocent*) was the most ingenious and ultimately the most futile enterprise of the early Cold War period. This involved tunnelling under the Soviet sector of the city to enable Western engineers to tap the telephone cables linking East Berlin with the Soviet Union and the countries of Eastern Europe. The cost, $25m, would have been considered prohibitive in any other era and it was not money well spent. It turned out that the master spy, George Blake, had let the Russians in on the secret from the start.

With the construction of the Wall and the growing East-West tensions that resulted, the stakes became higher and potentially lethal, providing writers with endless scenarios for dramatic spy novels, inspiring films like *Funeral in Berlin* (adapted from Len Deighton's novel) and Carol Reed's thriller, *The Man Between*. This is the twilight world that John Le Carré has made his own, a world where intelligence officers with all the paraphernalia of surveillance – telescopes, binoculars, directional microphones – squint into the cold night air waiting for the Soviet bloc defector to cross the arc-lit bridge to freedom while the Vopo sharpshooters await their orders.

Top right: Bahnhof
Friedrichstrasse
Above and right: Haus
am Checkpoint Charlie

GENDARMENMARKT

Once the site of a bustling market, the Gendarmenmarkt is named after an infantry regiment which was stationed here in the 18th century. (In the Communist era the square was known as Platz der Akademie.) Like neighbouring Bebelplatz, the existing layout of the square dates from the period of Frederick the Great and testifies to the contemporary obsession with making an 'Athens on the Spree'. In this case, however, the model is the Piazza del Popolo in Rome. Three architectural masterpieces overlook the square: the German and French Cathedrals (see pages 50 and 52), and Schinkel's magnificent Schauspielhaus (see page 98), completed in 1821. Outside the theatre a statue of Friedrich Schiller commemorates the great playwright's celebrated visit to Berlin in 1804, shortly before his death. It is a mark of Schiller's stature that German drama is, for the most part, performed on the square today and not the French comedies so assiduously promoted by Frederick the Great. However, the playwright most closely associated with Berlin, Heinrich von Kleist, has no memorial in the Gendarmenmarkt (see box). Another literary connection with the square is the writer E T A Hoffmann, whose fantastic stories inspired Offenbach's *Tales of Hoffmann*. A famous restaurant on the square, Lutter and Wegener, was the author's favourite haunt.

Mitte. U-Bahn to Französische Strasse.

GLIENICKER BRÜCKE AND SCHLOSS GLIENICKE

This unremarkable bridge across the Havel once marked the frontier between East and West and was the scene of dramatic spy swaps, notably the exchange, in 1962, of a Soviet agent for the American U-2 pilot, Gary Powers, shot down over Russia on a reconnaissance mission. The trade in human hostages, one of the harsher symptoms of the Cold War, seems a profanity in this idyllic natural setting. Protocol on such occasions demanded that representatives of both camps approach one another from their respective ends of the bridge, making towards a white painted line in the centre. Both prisoners had then to cross the border simultaneously. Meanwhile, plain clothes intelligence agents, diplomats and military figures with binoculars eyed the proceedings intently, watching for any trick or slip-up. The moment the prisoner made physical contact with someone from his own side, he was deemed to be safe. The Glienicke Bridge has long been of strategic importance. In 1945 it was blown up by advancing Soviet forces and subsequently rebuilt by the East German government which, either with calculated cynicism or indifference to irony, renamed it the Unity Bridge.

Set back from the road on the Wannsee bank is the Schloss Glienicke, a serene Italianate villa guarded by a pair of

Italianate Schloss Glienicke with splendid views across the River Havel

Schinkel's magnificent Schauspielhaus dominates the Gendarmenmarkt

HEINRICH VON KLEIST (1777–1811)

One of the most celebrated German Romantic writers, as much for the manner of his death as for his stories and plays, Kleist was brought up in the Prussian military tradition which he later unceremoniously rejected. His portrayal of the army in the play *The Prince of Homburg* made him a particular *bête noire* of Frederick William III, who outlawed his work, condemning him to a life of poverty. Ultimately driven to despair, he and his friend Henriette Vogel came to the wooded slopes of Wannsee and fulfilled a previously agreed suicide pact. Kleist's reputation was made overnight!

golden lions. It was built by Schinkel in 1826 for the brother of Kaiser Wilhelm I. The palace is closed to the public, but not the gardens, which were landscaped by the same Peter Lenné who designed both the park at Sanssouci and the Tiergarten. The gardens offer superb views of the Havel and the surrounding woodland, and contain a number of delightful arcadian follies, including a tea-house, rotunda and mock cloister, part of the fabric of which comes from a monastery in Venice. There is a restaurant with an outside terrace. *Zehlendorf, Königstrasse 36. Bus 116. Free entry to grounds.*

HANSAVIERTEL

This much vaunted housing development was the show-piece of the 1957 International Building Exhibition. More than 50 architects from all over the world contributed to the project, including the founder of the Bauhaus, Walter Gropius. The intention was to rejuvenate the northwestern edge of the Tiergarten, which had been devastated during World War II. The estate consists of a series of modest tower blocks and apartment buildings with conventional amenities (church, shops, nursery etc) and set in a landscaped environment. Once at the architectural cutting edge, it now looks distinctly dated.
Tiergarten, Altonaer Strasse. U-Bahn to Hansaplatz.

HAUS AM CHECKPOINT CHARLIE

The museum to the Berlin Wall is a stone's throw away from the famous crossing point where Soviet and American tanks once confronted each other. The prefabricated hut which served as a border post has been moved to the Museum für Verkehr und Technik (see page 78) but you can still see the red

A selection of military hats on sale at Checkpoint Charlie

and white barrier and the sign in four languages warning that 'You are leaving the American Sector'. The museum charts the history of the Wall but the

The 'Trabi' or Trabant car, a vivid reminder of East Berlin

emphasis is on escapology, the exhibits including hot-air balloons, cars with specially concealed compartments and other ephemera. While fun in an off-beat way, the museum appears vacuous, bearing in mind the tragic implications for the people of Berlin. Outside, an area fenced off by metal railings contains Wall paraphernalia, including sentry posts and rolls of barbed wire. It is possible to buy pieces of Wall here, too. But be warned: there are as many slabs of 'Wall' going the rounds as there were pieces of the true cross in the Middle Ages.
Kreuzberg, Friedrichstrasse 44. Tel: 2511031. Open: daily 9am–10pm. Admission charge. U-Bahn to Kochstrasse.

HUMBOLDT UNIVERSITÄT

This was originally a palace, designed by Johann Boumann between 1748 and 1753 for Frederick the Great's brother, Prince Heinrich, and intended as an element in the Forum Fredericianum. The university is named after the brothers Wilhelm and Alexander Humboldt, distinguished academics in their respective fields of philosophy and exploration. Statues of both men adorn the courtyard. Under Communist rule this was East Germany's leading institution of learning – highly convenient, as Karl Marx studied here from 1836 to 1841. (A new university for West Berliners was built in Dahlem.) Nowadays the city finds itself endowed with two centres of academic excellence.
Mitte, Unter den Linden. U-Bahn or S-Bahn to Friedrichstrasse.

KAISER WILHELM GEDÄCHTNISKIRCHE (Kaiser Wilhelm Memorial Church)

Only the blackened shell remains of this intended memorial to Kaiser Wilhelm I,

built in neo-Romanesque style between 1891 and 1895 by Franz Schwechten and bombed on the night of 22 November 1943. Its ruin has been preserved to commemorate the futility of war. An exhibition of photographs in the portico develops the theme. The ruined tower contrasts with two modern stained-glass buildings which reflect it, a bell-tower and an octagonal chapel with a strikingly beautiful interior. Berlin wits call the blackened ruin the jagged tooth, the chapel the make-up box and the tower the lipstick tube.
Charlottenburg, Breitscheidplatz. Tel: 2185023. Open: daily 9am–7pm. Memorial Hall – Tuesday to Saturday 10am–5pm. Free. U-Bahn or S-Bahn to Zoologischer Garten.

The Kaiser Wilhelm Church is now a monument to the futility of war

Mother with Child, drawing by the Berlin artist Käthe Kollwitz

KÄTHE-KOLLWITZ-MUSEUM

The life and work of the committed social artist, Käthe Kollwitz (1867–1945), are celebrated here. The setting, a handsome turn-of-the-century mansion in Charlottenburg, is hardly appropriate, bearing in mind that Kollwitz was moved to paint by the misery and hardship she observed in working class Prenzlauer Berg, where her husband was a doctor. After she lost a son during World War I the nightmare of war became an additional preoccupation. Kollwitz's socialist ideals did not endear her to the Nazis; her work was banned in 1936 and she was compelled to leave her post at the Academy of Arts. She died near Dresden a few days before the end of World War II.

The museum consists of paintings, woodcuts, charcoal drawings and sculptures created by Kollwitz during a prolific artistic career. The subjects are almost uniformly melancholic, but their underlying integrity makes them profoundly moving. Her studies of women, notably the sculpture *Muttergruppe*, emphasise collective strength in the face of unbearable hardship, while the striking poster, *Nie Wieder Krieg (Never Again War)*, and the cycle of woodcuts, both commemorating the death of her son Peter, reflect her lifelong pacifism.

Charlottenburg, Fasanenstrasse 24. Tel: 8825210. Open: daily except Tuesday 11am–6pm. Admission charge. U-Bahn to Kurfürstendamm.

KONGRESSHALLE

Berliners call this testament to German-US friendship the 'pregnant oyster', after the yawning cantilevered roof; in fact the architecture is meant to suggest the awnings of tents – funfairs and sideshows were held here in the past and Tent Street (In den Zelten) is just around the corner. Like a tent in the wind, Hugh Stubbins' roof collapsed in 1980 and had to be replaced. There are a number of sculptures in the garden, most notably *Large Butterfly* by Henry Moore. Also known as Haus der Kulturen der Welt (House of World Culture), the Kongresshalle stages temporary exhibitions.

Tiergarten, John-Foster-Dulles-Allee 10. Tel: 397870. Open: Tuesday to Thursday 2–6pm, Friday and Sunday 10am–8pm. Bus 100 to Kongresshalle.

KÖPENICK DISTRICT

There are currrently frenzied attempts to restore this attractive old town at the confluence of the Dahme and Spree rivers, the fabric of which was allowed to deteriorate by the East German government. Uncontrolled pollution from the neighbouring factory district and from heavy traffic did not help matters. Take a tolerant view, and you will find much charm among the potholes, cobbled streets and dilapidated orange trams.

To get to the old town, either take tram 86 or walk along Bahnhofstrasse, turning left at the junction with Lindenstrasse. Pass the park on the left and cross the Damm Bridge, where the River Dahme takes leave of the Spree. Köpenick received its charter in the 13th century when it was already a thriving market town and fishing village. Its character remained unchanged until the 19th century, when it acquired a sizeable factory suburb. Köpenick's workers fiercely resisted the Nazi takeover in 1933 and suffered for this in the Köpenicker Blutwoche (Week of Blood), when more than 90 Communists and Social Democrats were murdered. The red brick, neo-Gothic building with an impressive tower, dominating the narrow streets of the old town, is the Rathaus (Town Hall), complete with cellar restaurant.

Schloss Köpenick

Immediately beyond the old town is Schloss Köpenick. There has been a fortress here since the 9th century when the Slavs began colonising the area. The present building is Dutch baroque and was built in 1681 for the son of the Great Elector by Rutger van Langefelt. It now houses a small museum of decorative arts (Kunstgewerbemuseum Schloss Köpenick). More noteworthy is the Wappensaal, with its exquisite stuccoed ceiling, the work of the Italian Giovanni Carove, and the beautifully restored chapel, designed by Arnold Nering (one of the architects of Schloss Charlottenburg) in 1685.

S-Bahn to Köpenick, then tram 60, 61 or 62 to Schlossinsel. Open: Wednesday to Sunday 9am–5pm. Closed: Monday and Tuesday. Admission charge.

Berliners affectionately call the Kongresshalle the 'pregnant oyster'

Kulturforum

*T*his sprawling complex of museums and concert halls on the southern edge of the Tiergarten was conceived by Hans Scharoun in the early 1960s. The buildings, which seem to lack any sense of architectural unity, are grouped rather randomly around an isolated red and white brick church. This is the St Matthai-Kirche, designed in Italian Byzantine style by August Stüler in 1844, sole survivor of a once fashionable neighbourhood whose high society residents have been described in the novels of Theodor Fontane.

During the 1930s Hitler cleared much of the area as part of his plans for a grandiose North–South Axis running from near the Brandenburg Gate. Most of the former diplomatic quarter was removed, the exceptions being the Italian and Japanese embassies – now the Japanese-German Centre. Of the modern buildings the most eye-catching is the Philharmonie with its eccentric angles and gold cladding. The interior of the concert hall, home of the Berlin Philharmonic Orchestra, is well known for the quality of its acoustics. The Kulturforum is also home to the Kammermusiksaal (Chamber Concert Hall) and Staatsbibliothek (National Library), the Museum of Musical Instruments, the New National Gallery and the Museum of Applied Art (see below). From 1996 the new Gemäldegalerie and Kupferstichkabinett (paintings, prints and drawings) will be housed here.

KUNSTGEWERBEMUSEUM
(Museum of Applied Art)

The heartless exterior of this ugly red brick building, dating from 1978 to

Art deco stained glass in the Museum of Applied Art, Kulturforum

Exquisite Limoges vase, another modern art exhibit in the Kunstgewerbemuseum

1985, conceals a fine collection and a brilliant display. Inspired by the Victoria and Albert museum in London, it was founded in 1867 and contains the bulk of the pre-war national collection of applied art. (The remainder is in Köpenick.)

At the entrance level there is an information gallery where craft methods are explained in their historical context, a cafeteria and shop. In chronological sequence the museum begins one level below with a rich display of crosses, stained glass, caskets and ornate reliquaries, dating from medieval and Renaissance times. What makes the collection unique are the works of the medieval goldsmiths: the Dionysius Treasure of Enger-Herford which includes an exquisitely bejewelled 8th-century Burse reliquary said to have been produced for Charlemagne, and the 'Guelph Cross', part of the former treasure of the church of St Blasius, Braunschweig. Equally impressive are the baptismal bowl crafted for the Emperor Frederick Barbarossa and a 15th-century reliquary of St George slaying the dragon. On the same floor are Brussels tapestries, Venetian glass, Nuremberg silverware and Florentine majolica. The Lüneburg Town Hall Silver Plate (Lüneburger Ratssilber), dating from the 15th and 16th centuries, evokes the wealth of this distinguished Hanseatic port.

The collection resumes on the top floor with impressive displays of glass, silver, porcelain, stoneware, pewter and ivory. Perhaps the most interesting item here is the contents of the Pommersche Kunstschrank, an ebony cabinet destroyed by fire during World War II. Stuffed into the secret drawers and niches was a pot-pourri of precious objects, including surgical instruments,

Tiergarten, Kemperplatz. Museums open: Tuesday to Friday 9am–5pm, Saturday and Sunday 10am–5pm. Buses 129, 142, 148, 248, 341, 348. Near by: Bauhaus Archiv, Museum of German Resistance

hair brushes, games and miniature books, all made in Augsburg for the Duke of Pommern-Stettin in the early 17th century. The 18th-century porcelain is also worth seeing, especially Konrad Linck's grouping of Meleager and Atalante, produced in Frankenthal in 1778. All the major workshops are represented, among them Meissen, Nymphenburg and the Royal Porcelain Manufacturers of Berlin (KPM). Bringing the exhibition into the 20th century are sections devoted to Jugendstil/art nouveau glass and ceramics and art deco. An entertaining counterpoint to the craftsmanship of past ages is the display of modern domestic items in the basement, proving that even lowly objects like typewriters, telephones, kettles and hairdryers can be aesthetically pleasing.

Tel: 2662902/3. Admission charge.

Look but don't touch¹– musical instruments are also on show in the Kulturforum

MUSIKINSTRUMENTEN-MUSEUM

Tucked away behind the Philharmonie is the often neglected Museum of Musical Instruments, a branch of the Institute for Musical Research. The building was designed by Edgar Wisniewski in the early 1980s and is ideally suited to its purpose. Instruments are imaginatively laid out in spacious, well-lit galleries and are almost too accessible – avoid the temptation to touch, which immediately sets off an alarm! Altogether there are more than 2,200 items in the collection and each is lovingly maintained by the Institute's craft department. Occasionally one of the staff will give a demonstration but it is also possible to listen to sample performances on banks of headphones situated next to the display cases. The range of instruments is comprehensive – everything from ancient bagpipes, complete with animal bladders, to Stradivarius violins and the latest computer wizardry. There are harpsichords and claviers, each individually carved and hand-painted,

pianos of Beethoven vintage from the Berlin workshops of Kisting and Stöcker – including one with a double keyboard – and a Silbermann pianoforte similar to the one on which J S Bach played for Frederick the Great at Potsdam in 1747. A skilled musician himself, Frederick kept the instrument makers in business for more than 40 years: two transverse flutes from his personal collection are on permanent display. In the early 19th century, Berlin was a world leader in the manufacture of wind instruments. In 1818 production began of brass instruments with valves – an innovation which added immeasurably to the range and precision of horns, trumpets and trombones. The world's first bass tuba was also built in Berlin in 1835 by Johann Gottfried Moritz. The prize for the most bizarre contraption must go to the Orchestron, an enormous one-man-band of an organ kitted out with cymbals, drums, glockenspiel and whatever else the inventor could come up with.

Tel: 254810. Admission charge.

NEUE NATIONALGALERIE

The orientation of this challenging exhibition is towards international modern art, although 19th-century French and German painting is also well represented. *The Archer*, a sculpture in the garden by Henry Moore, sets the tone. Mies van der Rohe, a director of the Bauhaus who fled to the United States to escape Nazi persecution in 1938, designed the building with the distinctive black canopy which, back in the 1960s, was regarded as being in the vanguard of modernism. About half the museum space is taken up with temporary exhibitions, for which there is an extra charge. Some of these shows are spectacular so check with tourist information or the listings magazines.

One of the gallery's most appealing features is its roominess – it was designed with large canvases in mind. Wander through and admire the work of some of the leading artists of the post-war era, including Roy Lichtenstein, Robert Rauschenberg, Frank Stella and Joseph Beuys. But don't ignore the new generation of painters: Gerhard Richter's *Atelier* and Richard Lindner's witty *Arizona Girl*, both produced in the last decade, are a reminder that modern art can be stimulating and entertaining, as well as thought-provoking.

Step back in time by visiting the lower floor, where the focus is on French and German painting from the 19th and early 20th centuries. The most distinguished artists here are Adolph Menzel, Arnold Böcklin, Lovis Corinth, George Grosz and Otto Dix. Look out for Menzel's *Das Flötenkonzert* (The Flute Concert), a charming portrait of Frederick the Great playing the flute at Sanssouci; Böcklin's morose *Die Toteninsel* (*Island of the Dead*) and one of Grosz's most savage satires, *Pillars of Society*. The French school encompasses works from the Impressionists to Magritte: Monet's *St Germain l'Auxerrois* and Manet's *In the Winter Garden* are worth seeking out.

If the legs are giving out by this time, stop off at the Café Buchhandlung, which sells hot meals as well as light refreshment.

Tel: 2662650/1/3/4. Admission charge.

The Archer by British sculptor, Henry Moore, in the garden of the New National Gallery

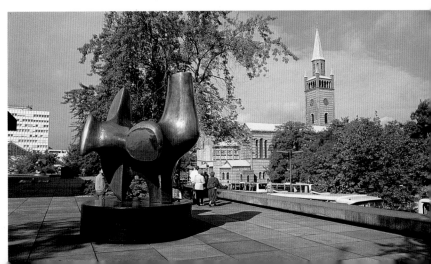

THE BERLIN PHILHARMONIC

If the players of the Berlin Philharmonic are virtuosi to a man and woman, the orchestra's fearsome reputation has derived equally from its principal conductors, all men of distinction, some of genius. Von Bülow, Nikisch, Furtwängler, Von Karajan... the list reads like a roll call of the great.

Below: The Philharmonie, home of the Berlin Philharmonic Orchestra (right)

Von Bülow, the world's first virtuoso conductor, became renowned for his flamboyance on the podium – a gift to cartoonists. His ability to conduct from memory was legendary: 'You should have the score in your head, not your head in the score', was his advice to a young protégé, the composer Richard Strauss. Under his successor, Arthur Nikisch, the orchestra became famous for its warm and impassioned performances. Tchaikovsky, several of whose works he premièred, was one of many to sing his praises.

The Berlin Philharmonic's association with the gramophone began before World War I with a recording by Von Bülow of Beethoven's *5th*

Symphony. But it was Nikisch's successor, Wilhelm Furtwängler, who began to exploit the medium, and the Berlin Philharmonic became renowned throughout the world for its performances of Beethoven, Bruckner and Wagner. After the Nazi seizure of power in 1933, Furtwängler and his orchestra were forced to tow the ideological line. The maestro ended the war hopelessly compromised and the orchestra, too, fell from grace.

Herbert von Karajan became maestro in 1954, and quickly re-established the orchestra's place on the world stage. Karajan promoted the cult of the maestro to the point where some

of his critics whispered darkly about megalomania. But to Berliners, who appreciated his contribution to the revitalisation of the city's cultural life after the war, and to music lovers everywhere, Von Karajan's genius as a conductor was undeniable. His death in July 1989 deprived the musical world of a colossus.

The orchestra has continued to be a formidable instrument in the hands of Claudio Abbado, whose style is more low-key than his predecessor's, but no less self-assured. The cult of the maestro may be disappearing but the signs are that the Berlin Philharmonic has once again fallen on its feet.

MARIENKIRCHE

The second oldest church in Berlin after the Nikolaikirche is a miraculous survivor of the heaviest bombing raid on the city, which occurred on the morning of 3 February 1945. Even more remarkable is the survival of the tower which had previously been destroyed by fire on no fewer than five occasions. The existing red brick structure is 15th-century German Gothic, while the present tower, with its distinctive lantern extension, dates from 1790 and is the work of Carl Gotthard Langhans, better known as the architect of the Brandenburg Gate. The interior is spacious, if a little shabby. Particularly noteworthy is the ornate baroque pulpit by Andreas Schlüter (1703). Near the tower is the *Totentanz* or *Dance of Death*, a medieval wall painting 22.6m long, commemorating an outbreak of plague in 1484. Bach played the organ in the Marienkirche in 1747 and today there are free recitals every Tuesday and Thursday at 2.30pm for 20 minutes.
Mitte, Neuer Markt. Tel: 2424467. Open: Monday to Thursday 10am–noon, 1–5pm; Saturday noon–4pm. Free. U-Bahn or S-Bahn to Alexanderplatz. Buses 100, 157, 348.

MÄRKISCHES MUSEUM

The only impressive feature of this museum is the building itself, a mock Gothic extravaganza designed for the municipal authorities in 1874. As an attempt to record the history of Berlin it is unimaginative and the surroundings are gloomy and oppressive. There are plans to combine the Märkisches Museum with the Berlin-Museum (see page 30).
Mitte, Am Köllnischen Park 5. Open: Wednesday to Sunday 10am–6pm. Admission charge. U-Bahn to Märkisches Museum or Jannowitzbrücke.

MARTIN-GROPIUS-BAU

Designed in the style of the Italian Renaissance, this building dates from 1877 and is the work of Martin Gropius, uncle of Walter, founder of the Bauhaus Movement. The interior is spacious and lavish, a courtyard covered by a glass dome, with gilded arcades, richly decorated ceilings, mosaics and chandeliers. Art exhibitions are held here from time to time.
Kreuzberg, Stresemannstrasse 110. Tel: 254860. Open: daily 10am–8pm. Closed: Monday. Admission charge.

Miraculous survivor of World War II bombing – the Marienkirche

Designed in the 19th century, the façade of the Martin-Gropius-Bau is in Italian Renaissance style

MITTE DISTRICT

The Mitte, literally 'middle', is the historic centre of Berlin. The twin medieval settlements of Berlin-Cölln grew up on the banks of the Spree near Museum Island. The town gradually extended to include the Nikolaiviertel and the neighbourhood of the Marienkirche. Beginning in the 17th century, the old fortifications were torn down and replaced with squares and gardens, while three new suburbs were added: Friedrichswerder, Dorotheenstadt and Friedrichstadt. In the period of renewed confidence following the defeat of Napoleon, the city was embellished with fine neo-classical buildings, many the work of Berlin's greatest architect, Karl Friedrich Schinkel. After World War I, the westward expansion of the city accelerated but Friedrichstrasse, Leipzigerstrasse and Potsdamer Platz remained important centres for business and entertainment. The Mitte was reduced to ruins by bombing during World War II – the Reich Chancellery and the Military High Command were located here. Since 1989 attempts have been made to reintegrate the Mitte with the West End and to inject new life.

MOABIT DISTRICT

The area north of the Tiergarten became a centre of industry in the mid-19th century, after the Borsig locomotive works had moved here from Kreuzberg. The tenement blocks around Beusselstrasse, though now spruced up, are a reminder of Moabit's working class past. For Berliners Moabit will always be associated with prisons: the gaol on Turmstrasse, which features in Alfred Döblin's novel *Berlin Alexanderplatz*, no longer functions but Plötzensee, notorious under the Nazis, still exists as a youth reformatory and there is a women's prison near by. Nowadays industrial Moabit is confined to the area around the Westhafen docks, though even here stretches of the Spree can be surprisingly scenic.

Minor Museums and Galleries

Of the approximately 150 museums and galleries in Berlin these are some that are often overlooked:

BERLIN SATIRE MUSEUM

A thoroughly entertaining and neatly packaged tramp through the history of circus, variety and cabaret. Numerous programmes, photographs, posters, costumes and other *memorabilia* and friendly, interested staff.
Wallstrasse/Inselstrasse 7. Tel: 2792165. Open: Wednesday to Sunday 10am–6pm. Admission charge. U-Bahn to Märkisches Museum. Buses 142, 257.

CHARLOTTENBURG HEIMAT MUSEUM (Charlottenburg Local Museum)

Maps, photographs and models trace the history and development of this famous Berlin district, once a rural backwater but transformed at the turn of the century into a thriving commercial and residential area with a population that increased from 30,000 to 300,000 in the space of three decades.
Schlossstrasse 69. Tel: 34303201. Open: Tuesday to Friday 10am–5pm; Sunday 11am–5pm. Free. Buses 109, 110, 145.

DEUTSCHES RUNDFUNK-MUSEUM (German Museum of Broadcasting)

Located in a former studio at the base of the Radio Tower (Funkturm), the museum displays wirelesses from the 1920s and '30s and a reconstructed radio shop from the same period. The tower is no longer used for its original purpose but visitors may take the lift to the observation platform (138m) for dizzying views over Charlottenburg.
Messedamm. Tel: 3028186. Open: daily except Tuesday 10am–5pm. Admission charge. S-Bahn to Westkreuz. Buses 104, 149, 219.

FRISEURMUSEUM (Museum of Hairdressing)

Displays on changing hair fashions as well as some unbelievably ponderous equipment. The museum is in Prenzlauer Berg, on the same street as the Museum of Working Class Life.
Husemannstrasse 8. Tel: 4495380. Open: Monday and Saturday 10am–6pm, Tuesday to Thursday 10am–5pm, Sunday 10am–4pm. Admission charge. U-Bahn to Eberswalder Strasse.

MUSEUM BERLINER ARBEITERLEBEN UM 1900 (Museum of Berlin Working Class Life around 1900)

One of the once notorious tenement blocks known as *Mietskasernen* (rent barracks) houses this exhibition on working class life, which begins with a review of the former East German Government's attempts to project a vision of a New German Working Man. A reconstructed flat is furnished as it might have been at the turn of the century: the rooms are cramped and the furnishings modest, but there is little sense here of the airlessness and lack of light typical of the *Mietskasernen*, where most of the apartments backed on to a series of gloomy *Hinterhöfe* or backyards.

Husemannstrasse 12. Tel: 4485675. Open: Tuesday to Saturday 10am–6pm (Friday 3pm). Admission charge. U-Bahn to Eberswalder Strasse.

OTTO-NAGEL-HAUS

An exhibition of the work of noted Communist artists like Otto Nagel (1894–1967), Käthe Kollwitz and Otto Dix. Whether the museum survives in its present form, given the changing political climate, is an open question.
Mitte, Märkisches Ufer 16. Tel: 2791424. Open: Wednesday to Sunday 9am–5pm. Admission charge. U-Bahn to Märkisches Museum.

PANOPTIKUM (Waxworks Museum)

Children will enjoy this traditional favourite, situated in the centre of town.
Charlottenburg, Ku'damm Eck/ Joachimsthaler Strasse, 3rd floor. Tel: 8839000. Open: daily 10am–11pm. Admission charge. U-Bahn to Kurfürstendamm.

POSTMUSEUM BERLIN
(Postal Museum)

An engaging display of franking machines, old mail boxes, stamps and other postal paraphernalia. The star of the show is the collection of prototype telephones from the late 19th century.
Schöneberg, An der Urania 15. Tel: 21711717. Open: Monday to Thursday 9am–5pm, Saturday and Sunday 10am–5pm. Free. U-Bahn to Wittenbergplatz. Buses 109, 119, 129, 146, 185.

TEDDY MUSEUM BERLIN

A port of call for the very young or the young at heart. Paddington, Winnie and Rupert are all to be found here, as are some very old bears – almost as old, in

fact, as the century itself.
Kurfürstendamm Karree/Uhlandstrasse, 1st floor. Open: daily except Tuesday 3pm–10pm. Free. U-Bahn to Uhlandstrasse.

ZILLE-MUSEUM

An exhibition of paintings, drawings, sketches and cartoons by one of the century's wittiest and most engaging social satirists, Heinrich Zille (1858–1929). The location is a reconstructed apothecary's shop.
Mitte, Bahnhof Friedrichstrasse. Tel: 2082590. Open: daily except Tuesday 11am–6pm. Free. U-Bahn or S-Bahn to Friedrichstrasse.

Theatrical costumes add to the colour of the Berlin Satire Museum

Museumsinsel

*M*useum Island was conceived in the 1820s as a sanctum for the educated citizen to reflect on the artistic achievements of the classical past. It was a new idea but not one confined to Prussia – the British Museum in London dates from the same period, and Napoleon had already exhibited the plunder from his conquests to an enthusiastic public in Paris.

To house the collection, which was based on the Prussian royal family's Chamber of Antiquities, part of the Spree was drained and a classical temple commissioned from the great architect K F Schinkel. But when the museum opened in 1830 the contents seemed too paltry for the monumental surroundings. With this in mind Schinkel and fellow sculptor Daniel Rauch travelled to Italy and Greece on the look-out for likely purchases. They were assisted by academics like Wilhelm von Humboldt,

who advised on the merits of the various private collections on offer. But the biggest contribution was made by the archaeologist Carl Richard Lepsius who, profiting from the naïvety of the Ottoman ruler of Egypt, amassed a hoard of neglected treasures. There was now an embarrassment of riches and more museum space was needed. The Neues Museum was opened in 1855 and the Nationalgalerie in 1876.

Spurred on by the prospect of more empty rooms and by a belief in Germany's civilising mission, the archaeologists went to work with a vengeance. Heinrich Schliemann's exciting discoveries at Troy were followed by equally rewarding excavations at Olympia in Greece and Pergamon (Bergama) in Turkey, where Carl Humann was in the process of recovering the famous altar. The culmination was Robert Koldewey's expedition of 1899–1912, which uncovered the awe-inspiring treasures of Babylon. By the time the host countries were alerted to what they were losing and had begun to restrict the export of antiquities, the Germans had secured a stupendous haul.

Until the outbreak of World War II, it was possible for visitors to Berlin to review a succession of ancient

Ernst von Ihne's Bode-Museum dominates the Spree from Museum Island

Larger than life – the breathtaking Pergamon altar in the museum of the same name

civilisations simply by walking the length of Museum Island. But the war had a disastrous impact on all the Berlin collections. Many of the treasures were looted by the occupying Soviet forces and taken to Moscow, where they have only recently re-emerged. Others ended up in the hands of the Allies and are currently housed in Dahlem and Charlottenburg. There are now plans to merge these collections with those of Museum Island but the logistics are formidable and the situation will not be resolved until early in the next century. No visit to Berlin is complete without a visit to Museum Island, especially the Pergamon. Guides and plans are on sale at the bookshop and each suite of rooms contains perspex pouches with fact sheets on the relevant exhibits (sometimes in English). Bear in mind that for some time to come the contents of the museums will remain in a state of flux.

Mitte. Tel: 203550. S-Bahn to Hackescher Markt or Friedrichstrasse. Buses 100, 157, 348.

MUSEUMSINSEL

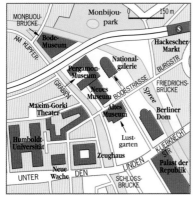

For Schinkel, the Rotunda in the Altes Museum was a sanctuary for exhibiting precious objects

who financed Berlin's first public museum. The building took six years to complete and originally housed the Kaiser's modest collection of paintings and sculptures. Not content with the overwhelming impression made by the façade, Schinkel has a surprise in store: hidden in the core of the building is a Rotunda inspired, like St Hedwigs Kathedrale (see page 84), by the Pantheon in Rome. For Schinkel this was the 'sanctuary' where the most precious objects were to be revered. Statues of the gods surround the visitor between the columns on ground level and in the ambulatory above, while natural light streams in from the roof to reveal the cofferwork of the dome. The museum is currently used for major temporary exhibitions and international art shows. *Special exhibitions only: 9am–5pm (closed Monday, Tuesday). Admission charge.*

ALTES MUSEUM

To receive the full impact of this magnificent building it is necessary to approach it from the vast, tree-colonnaded space of the Lustgarten. One of Schinkel's great masterpieces, the Altes Museum is his homage to classical architecture and a powerful reminder of his vision of Berlin as 'Athens on the Spree'. On climbing the imposing staircase, the visitor encounters a façade 87m long, the expanse broken evenly by 18 massive Ionic columns supporting an entablature crowned with brooding imperial eagles and an inscription in gold lettering to Kaiser Friedrich Wilhelm III,

BODE-MUSEUM

The best view of this handsome building, surrounded on three sides by the River Spree, is from the Monbijou Bridge. It was built by Ernst Eberhard von Inhe from 1897 to 1904 and its neo-baroque design, with a distinctive dome, breaks the classical convention set by the other buildings on the island. Though all the collections are depleted, the museum is well worth a look. The interior is spectacular, with sweeping staircases, balustrades and marble colonnaded halls. On the ground floor are stone sculptures (*Skulpturensammlung*) – mainly damaged statues salvaged from the ruins of various Berlin buildings at the end of the war. There are also medieval wooden sculptures, notably by 15th-century sculptor Tilman Riemenschneider. The Far East collection (*Fernostsammlung*) has art from China, Japan and Korea.

The Egyptian collection (*Ägyptische Sammlung*), though inferior to its twin in Charlottenburg, has an interesting collection of mummies, sarcophagi and statues, though the presentation is rather old-fashioned. On the first floor are collections of coins (*Münzkabinett*), early Christian and Byzantine art (*Frühchristliche-byzantische Sammlung*), including a 6th-century mosaic fragment of Christ and the saints from the church of San Michele in Ravenna, and the picture gallery (*Gemäldegalerie*), comprising minor German and Flemish works.
Open: 9am–5pm (closed Monday, Tuesday). Admission charge.

NATIONALGALERIE
Designed by Friedrich August Stüler in the neo-classical style in 1867, the Nationalgalerie was established to display contemporary German art. (A famous retrospective exhibition in 1906 introduced the German public to its rich 19th-century heritage.) Unfortunately, most of the best work is now dispersed or in private hands. But it is worth looking out for paintings by Adolph Menzel and especially for the collection of modern seccessionist and expressionist art. The display varies, but you may see works by Lovis Corinth, Lesser Ury, Max Liebermann and Ernst Ludwig Kirchner.
Open: 9am–5pm (closed Monday, Tuesday). Admission charge.

NEUES MUSEUM
This neo-classical building, dating from 1843 to 1855, was designed by August Stüler for the Egyptian collection. His original idea, that the wall paintings and décor should harmonise with the contents of the rooms to create a whole work of art, turned out to be impractical. The museum is closed for restoration for the foreseeable future.

Athens on the Spree – Berlin's neo-classical National Gallery

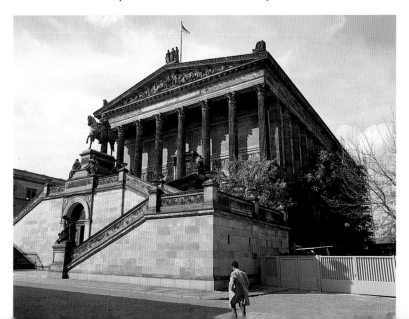

PERGAMON-MUSEUM

A marvellous survey of the art and architecture of the ancient world, from Babylon through Sumeria, Assyria and Mesopotamia to classical Greece and Rome. Pass through the foyer directly into Hall I and feast your eyes on the exhibit which gives the museum its name, the Pergamon Altar. Pergamon (Bergama) lies near the western coast of modern Turkey and was once one of the most important centres of the Hellenistic world. Much of the history of the Pergamons is shrouded in obscurity but it is known that in 165BC they overcame their Galatean enemies after a prolonged war. This victory is commemorated in the frieze commissioned by King Eumenes II: the battle of the gods and the giants, which can be seen around the walls of the hall. At 120m, it is the largest continuous band of frieze in existence with the exception of the Parthenon in Athens. A model of the acropolis of Pergamon sets the altar in its original context of temples, library, royal palaces and theatre. The altar was discovered during excavations supervised by the archaeologist Carl Humann from 1878 to 1886. Centuries earlier it had been described by the Roman writer Lucius Ampelius as a wonder of the world.

Hall II contains other outstanding pieces of Hellenistic architecture, including a portico from the temple of Athena in Pergamon. Hall III, on the other side of the Altar, contains a reconstruction of the gateway of the market place in Miletus (western Turkey). Built in AD120 under the Emperor Hadrian, it was excavated by Humann's successor, Theodor Wiegand, between 1899 and 1913. Once the gateway to the city's southern market, it was originally framed by impressive public buildings. In the 6th century AD the Emperor Justinian incorporated the gateway into the city wall. It was later destroyed in an earthquake and had to be pieced together fragment by fragment.

Pass through one gateway into another: the Ishtar Gate from Babylon. Nebuchadnezzar II, who commissioned it, predicted rightly that it would be something 'upon which humankind in its entirety will gaze with wonder'. It was built between 604 and 562BC and is dedicated to the weather god Adad, whose symbol was the bull, and Marduk, patron of the city, represented by dragons. Ishtar, after whom the gate is named, was the goddess of war – her symbol is the lion. This reconstructed gate is only a section: people entering by this, one of seven gates in the double walled fortifications of the city, would have had to pass through a portal 48m

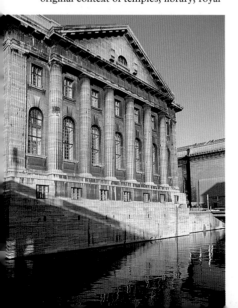

No visit to Berlin would be complete without a trip to the Pergamon-Museum

To the Babylonians, the lion was the symbol of the goddess of war

thick. The processional way, which is also reconstructed in the museum, was originally 20m wide and 250m long and played an important part in religious ceremonial.

Rooms leading off the processional way form part of the Middle Eastern department and include stone vases and animal figurines from Sumeria, a sceptre from Babylon, cuneiform tablets from Assyria, glazed stone reliefs from Persia and artefacts from excavations at Megiddo and Jericho. A wonderful collection of Greek and Roman statues can be approached from Hall II. The most precious are the Greek originals, including an incomplete mask from Marathon (dating from 470BC) and a terracotta figure of a Boeotian woman with sunhat and fan which still shows traces of the original gold, red and blue paint. Among the Roman exhibits, particularly noteworthy is the famous Berlin bust of the Emperor Caracalla (AD212–17), showing a man of stern and irritable disposition.

The highlight of the Department of Islamic Art on the upper floor is a segment of the wall of the palace of Mshatta, a desert fortress of the Caliphs of the 8th-century Umayyad dynasty.
Open: 9am–5pm (Monday, Tuesday only main rooms). Admission charge.

Classical sculptures abound in the Pergamon-Museum

An amazing Aladdin's cave for the technologically minded

MUSEUM FÜR VERKEHR UND TECHNIK (Museum of Transport and Technology)

As the giant mural on the Landwehr Canal promises, this is an Aladdin's cave for anyone with an interest in steam trains, bi-planes, vintage cars, bicycles, sailing ships and all kinds of industrial machinery and paraphernalia. With its accent on hands-on experience, the science museum is also ideal for children, but be warned – the collection can be overwhelming, so it's probably best to concentrate on areas which have greatest appeal.

The museum has the perfect home – long abandoned industrial buildings, including the former workshops and locomotive sheds of the old Anhalter Bahnhof, Berlin's southern railway terminus, built in 1840 but demolished in the 1950s (part of the ruined façade can still be seen across the river on the corner of Schöneberger Strasse).

The ground floor exhibits include historic aircraft like the 1917 Fokker triplane and 1941 Junkers Ju 52; vintage cars in pristine condition, among them models designed by the pioneers Gottlieb Daimler and Karl Benz; buses, motor cycles and a 1904 fire engine. The Versuchsfeld (experiment room) offers the chance to operate buttons and gadgets, while programmed computers play chess or music. The old locomotive sheds are an ideal setting for the steam trains, coaches, turntables and scale models. Upstairs, in the former manager's office, are models of the first German iron and steel ships, as well as locks and bridges.

There is a period café and a bookshop with postcards of old Berlin for sale.
Kreuzberg, Trebbiner Strasse 9. Tel: 254840. Open: Tuesday to Friday 9am–5.30pm, Saturday and Sunday 10am–6pm. Admission charge. U-Bahn to Möckernbrücke or Gleisdreieck. Bus 129.

MUSEUMSDORF DÜPPEL

This open-air museum in the Zehlendorf district is on the site of a medieval village and reconstructs life as it might have been lived here in the 12th century. Its atmosphere is relaxed and friendly and there are demonstrations of handicrafts like spinning, weaving and pottery and farming techniques. The museum is difficult to reach without a car; note also the restricted opening times.

The Grunewald forest and the resort of Wannsee are both within striking distance.
Zehlendorf, Clauerstrasse 11. Tel: 8026671. Open: May to September, Thursday 3–7pm; Sunday and holidays 10am–5pm. Admission charge. Buses 115, 211.

NEUE SYNAGOGE

Standing in the heart of the old Jewish quarter, this remarkable building, easily identified by its gleaming onion domes, may once again become the focus of Jewish community life. It was built by two distinguished architects, neither of them Jews, Eduard Knoblauch and August Stüler, and opened in 1866 in the presence of Kaiser Wilhelm I and his prime minister, Otto von Bismarck. The synagogue is large (there is room for 3,000 worshippers), and its design is unashamedly exotic and eclectic – a heady brew of Moorish and Byzantine influences executed in yellow brick. Listed building status protected the synagogue from the worst excesses of the Nazi's 'night of broken glass' (*Reichskristallnacht*), 9 November 1938, when all other Jewish monuments and places of worship were destroyed. Ironically, Allied bombs finally devastated the building, which was at the time being used as an ammunition store. A plaque on the wall of the reconstructed synagogue admonishes visitors: 'never forget'. From 1995, if all goes well, it will function again as a place of worship and will also be a centre for Jewish studies (*Centrum Judaicum*). But it is a sad reflection of the times that a policeman guards the entrance.

Near by, in Grosse Hamburger Strasse, is the Old Jewish Cemetery, dating from 1672, when immigrants began arriving from Vienna. Although the cemetery was no longer in use by the time the Nazis came to power, it was desecrated and subsequently destroyed by the Gestapo in 1943.
Oranienburger Strasse 30. U-Bahn to Friedrichstrasse or S-Bahn to Oranienburger Strasse.

The gleaming onion dome of the New Synagogue is a burning landmark

...IE (New Watch)

...al guardhouse (the Palace ...osite) was built to a classical design by Schinkel in 1818 to complement the baroque Zeughaus or Arsenal (now the German Historical Museum) which stands next to it. The ceremony of the changing of the guard began here in the 19th century. After World War I the guardhouse became a monument to Germany's unknown soldier and, after World War II, a 'Memorial to the Victims of Fascism and Militarism'. However, the irony of goose-stepping East German soldiers carrying out their ceremonial duties here was not lost on Berliners, who referred to them as 'Red Prussians'. The soldiers disappeared with the army in which they served in 1990.
Unter den Linden.

Berlin's oldest congregational church, the Gothic Nikolaikircke

NIKOLAIKIRCHE (St Nicholas Church)

This is Berlin's oldest parish church. A Romanesque basilica stood on the site until 1200, when work on the present building commenced. The Gothic choir and nave were completed in 1470; in 1879 Hermann Blankenstein replaced the tower with two thrusting spires. It was here that the hitherto separate communities of Berlin and Cölln agreed to join in 1307; here, too, that Protestantism was welcomed by Bishop Buchholzer in 1539, a little more than 20 years after Luther's first adversary, the Dominican monk, Johannes Tetzel, had preached the need for Catholic reform from the same pulpit. The church is now a museum of the early history of Berlin.
Mitte, Nikolaikirchplatz. Tel: 2380900. Open: Tuesday to Sunday 10am–6pm. Closed: 4pm if concert on. Admission charge. U-Bahn or S-Bahn to Alexanderplatz.

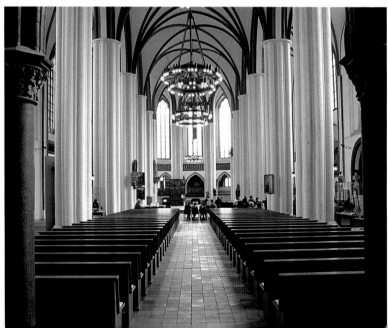

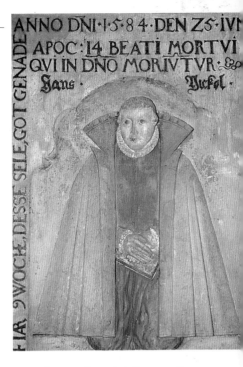

Renaissance effigy in the Nikolaikirche, one of many interesting exhibits on show

POTSDAMER PLATZ

The fate of this once famous square is now sealed. In October 1993 work finally began on an enormous new development for one of Germany's most prestigious firms, Daimler-Benz. Their customer services division will occupy more than half the site at an estimated cost of 3 billion DM. The project is a controversial one: Daimler bought the site shortly after the Wall came down and before there had been any time for consultation. Potsdamer Platz was once Berlin's most important traffic intersection, bounded by hotels, restaurants and night spots and served by the grandiose Potsdam Railway Station. But it was also perilously close to army headquarters and the Reich Chancellery. During the war Allied bombing erased it from the map, determining its fate for the next 50 years.
S-Bahn to Potsdamer Platz.

REICHSTAG (Parliament)

One of Berlin's most distinctive landmarks and a potent symbol of its troubled history, the parliament building is about to gain a new lease of life, following the decision in June 1991 to move the German seat of government back to Berlin from Bonn by the year 2000. The Reichstag was designed by Paul Wallot in 1884 and completed 10 years later; its shallow dome had to be dismantled for safety after World War II. Although an inscription on one of the external walls dedicates it to the German people, the Reichstag's associations with democratic government are ambiguous, to say the least. Before World War I it was effectively the Prussian aristocracy,

not parliament, that ruled Germany. In November 1918 the republic was proclaimed from the Reichstag but little more than a year later conditions verging on civil war forced the new national assembly to meet in the small provincial town of Weimar. In February 1933 the Nazis used the excuse of the Reichstag being set on fire to do away with parliament altogether.

In 1992 the government launched a competition for a revitalised Reichstag building. British architect Sir Norman Foster's winning design envisages retaining the original shell while transforming the interior into a vast concourse with easy public access to the chamber.
Tiergarten, Platz der Republik. Tel: 39770.
Open: Tuesday to Sunday 10am–5pm.
Free. S-Bahn to Unter den Linden.
Buses 100, 248.

WHITHER BERLIN?

'**B**erlin is always becoming, never being' said the art critic Karl Scheffler in 1910. The remark is as true today as it was then. Berlin is never content with standing still. There are currently more than 20 major areas of redevelopment in greater Berlin, from Pankow in the north to Treptow in the south; from Charlottenburg in the west to Köpenick in the east. Perhaps the crane and the bulldozer, rather than the bear, should be the city's twin symbols.

By the turn of the century Berlin will be the centre of government as well as the capital of a united Germany. The sensitivities of both East and West have to be borne in mind; so while many of the new ministries will be housed in the vicinity of Alexanderplatz, parliament itself will convene in the rejuvenated Reichstag.

Commercial redevelopment is a priority in the East. The massive complex at Friedrichstadt Passage, due to open in 1995, will combine shops with restaurants, offices, apartments and galleries. But the trendy boutiques, designer cafés and computer hardware stores opening up on Unter den Linden are way beyond the pocket of the average East Berliner. To encourage visitors to stray east of the Brandenburg Gate, a new underground line is being built to link the Ku'damm with Friedrichstrasse and Alexanderplatz.

Berliners take a keen interest in the future of their city and many of the proposed developments have aroused fierce controversy. Unfortunately, in the present recessionary climate, financial considerations

the Palast der Republik, the grotesque Communist showpiece which currently occupies the site. Berlin has always had a problem with identity: 'Berlin is a great city, a world city (perhaps?)' wrote Kaiser Wilhelm II before World War I. Looking to the future, the new tourist chief has declared his intention: to remove the query and to make Berlin undeniably a world city, on a par with London, Paris, Rome or New York.

Looking to the future – the face of Berlin is constantly changing

are paramount and public consultation little more than a formality. A good example of this was Daimler-Benz's acquisition of much of Potsdamer Platz for offices before alternative proposals to recreate the glitzy atmosphere of pre-war days could be considered.

Greater sensitivity has been shown in deciding the future of the Lustgarten. In the summer of 1993 a highly entertaining and imaginative exhibition became the vehicle for debating whether to rebuild Schlüter's baroque masterpiece, the Schloss. But the cost of such a venture will surely be prohibitive. For the moment the discussion has shifted to deciding the fate of

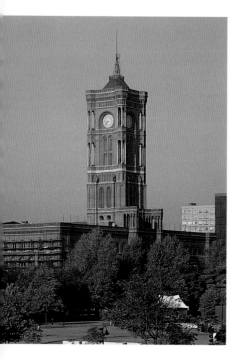

Berlin's Red Town Hall is the symbol of a
newly-unified community

SACHSENHAUSEN
See pages 110–11.

ST-HEDWIGS-KATHEDRALE
Berlin's Roman Catholic cathedral was
inspired by the Roman Pantheon (the
interior does bear a passing resemblance)
– or was it an upturned coffee cup which
influenced Frederick the Great's choice
of design? The church was built between
1747 and 1783 by Knobelsdorff and
Johann Boumann but the outsize green
dome, which distracts from the fine
pediment and massive Ionic columns,
was not completed until the end of the
19th century. For a long time this was
the only Catholic place of worship in this
overwhelmingly Protestant city.
*Mitte, Bebelplatz. Tel: 2034810. Open:
Monday to Saturday 10am–5pm, Sunday
1–5pm. Free. U-Bahn to Hausvogteiplatz.
Buses 100, 147, 157, 257, 348.*

ROTES RATHAUS (Red Town Hall)
Named for the colour of the brick, not
the politics of the city fathers, the 100m-
high tower is an unmistakeable landmark
for Berlin's residents. It was completed
in 1869 from a design by Heinrich
Friedrich Waesemann and is loosely
modelled on the Renaissance town halls
of northern Italy. When the city was
divided, the Rotes Rathaus appropriately
became the municipal headquarters of
East Berlin, while the West adopted
Rathaus Schöneberg. The Rotes Rathaus
now serves both communities once
more. There are plans to open a
restaurant in the cellar, as is traditional
with German town halls.
*Alexanderplatz/Spandauer Strasse. S-Bahn
to Alexanderplatz.*

SCHEUNENVIERTEL
Lying just to the north of Museum
Island and Monbijou Park, the 'barn
quarter' of Berlin was where Jewish
migrants settled in the 1670s after the
Great Elector Frederick William offered
them a safe haven from persecution in
Austria. (The gesture was not an
altruistic one – the refugees were
expected to bring their considerable
wealth with them.) During the relatively
tolerant 18th century the community
thrived and, through distinguished
leaders like Moses Mendelssohn, made
an important contribution to the
commercial and cultural life of the city.
By 1850 the wealthier families were
moving into more salubrious parts of the
city, while the Scheunenviertel

deteriorated into the slum that Theodore Fontane has described in his novels. Despite this, tradition determined that the prestigious New Synagogue was built here in the 1860s (see page 79). By 1910 Jews were as well represented in Berlin as the Turks are today. It was this prominence, coupled with envy at the distinction they had achieved in every walk of life from journalism and publishing to science and banking, that brought them to the attention of racist ideologues. When the Nazis came to power in 1933 the party's propaganda chief, Joseph Goebbels, made a particular point of equating the appalling living conditions and criminal reputation of the Scheunenviertel with the Jewish presence. The New Synagogue was one of many throughout the city attacked on *Reichskristallnacht* (9 November 1938), after which the fate of the Jews was sealed. From 1942 more than 55,000 Berlin Jews were taken to an old people's home on Grosse Hamburger Strasse before being transported to Auschwitz and other extermination camps. (A monument to the victims of fascism stands on the site.) Today there are only 5,000 Jews in Berlin but the synagogue survives, as does the site of the Old Jewish Cemetery, which was desecrated by the Nazis. The heart of this interesting quarter, Oranienburger Strasse, is still rather run down but there is an undercurrent of '60s radical chic. *S-Bahn to Hackescher Markt.*

SCHLOSS BABELSBERG

King Friedrich Wilhelm III commissioned Karl Friedrich Schinkel to design a summer residence for his family in 1833. At the request of his wife, it was modelled on Britain's Windsor Castle, which the couple had visited a few years earlier. The neo-Gothic Schloss was subsequently enlarged to accommodate a greater number of guests. The fabulous park with views across the Havel towards Potsdam, Schloss Glienicke and the Glienicke Bridge, was laid out by Peter Joseph Lenné and Hermann Puckler-Muskau in 1833–5. Perched on the water's edge is the Kleines Schloss (Small Castle), built in 1841 for Princess Augusta's ladies-in-waiting. Schloss Babelsberg was a favourite with the King for the remainder of his life. Most of the leading politicians of the day attended him here at some time or other, including the 'Iron Chancellor', Bismarck, on the occasion of his appointment as Minister President of Prussia in 1862 – an event with profound consequences for the future of Germany.

Potsdam, Auf dem Babelsberg. Admission charge. Bus 116 or 216 to Schloss Glienicke, then walk or take bus 691.

Royal retreat – neo-Gothic Schloss Babelsberg, modelled on Windsor Castle

Schloss Charlottenburg

*T*his exquisite palace, belonging to the Prussian royal house of Hohenzollern, has been miraculously recreated from the original plans after being almost totally destroyed in World War II.

Charlottenburg was a bucolic Eden in 1695 when the cultivated Electoress Sophie Charlotte, a noted patron of artists and philosophers, commissioned Arnold Nering to design her a modest rural retreat between Berlin and Potsdam. The enhanced status of the Hohenzollerns after 1701, when the Elector became King Frederick I of Prussia, was reflected in the enlargement of house and grounds under the supervision of Johann Eosander Göthe. The transformation of the palace into a miniature Versailles was the brainchild of Frederick the Great, who instructed the inspired architect Georg Wenzeslaus von Knobelsdorff, a retired captain in the Prussian army, to build an entire new wing in rococo style, including a suite of royal apartments. Carl Gottfried Langhans designed the theatre at the western end of the Orangery and the tea house in the grounds, now known as the Belvedere (1788). Finally, in 1810, Friedrich Wilhelm III chose to honour the memory of his popular wife, Queen Luise, by commissioning a mausoleum from Karl Friedrich Schinkel, who also had a hand in designing new living quarters at the eastern end of the New Wing.

The encroachment of the city has unfortunately foreshortened the approach to the palace, but it is still impressive. An equestrian statue by Andreas Schlüter, representing the Great Elector in characteristically martial mood, dominates the courtyard. It originally stood on the Lange Brücke outside the Berlin Schloss. Visitors are taken on a conducted tour of the ground floor apartments of the Old Wing which lasts approximately one hour. The tasteful elegance of the Gobelin rooms with their magnificent tapestries, delicately painted harpsichords and French paintings, the red braid room, a dazzling spectacle of damask and gilded stucco, and the porcelain chamber with its magnificent painted ceiling all serve as a reminder that there was more to the Prussian monarchy than blustering ambition and military aggrandisement. The highlights of the New Wing, on the eastern side of the palace, are the breath-taking Golden Gallery, a rococo masterpiece, and the equally sumptuous White Hall, both designed for Frederick the Great. It is easy to imagine Frederick playing the flute in these refined surroundings, accompanied on the harpsichord by the most talented of Bach's sons, Carl Philip Emmanuel. Queen Luise's bedroom, designed

Schloss Charlottenburg, one of Berlin's architectural gems

by Schinkel, is also on the first floor and there are paintings of the French 18th-century school, including Watteau's *Departure for Cythera* and works by Boucher and Pesne.

On the western side of the building is the Great Orangery, now used for exhibitions, and the sedate Langhans Building, a museum of pre- and early history. Directly behind it, an avenue of fir trees leads to the Mausoleum. This is the burial place of a number of Prussian rulers and their subjects, including Kaiser Wilhelm I and Queen Luise, whose tomb, by Christian Daniel Rauch, is in impeccable taste.

The landscaped English Garden unrolls park-like into the distance. Far to the right, on the banks of the Spree, is the compact Belvedere, designed by Langhans. It is now a museum of the history of Berlin porcelain, with high quality pieces from the factories of Wegely, Gotzkowsky and the Royal Porcelain Manufacturers (KPM). The formal French Garden, with its sculpted lawns, shrubs, lakes and fountains, begins behind the green cupola of the palace. To the east is the Galerie der Romantik and the Schinkel-Pavillon, with 19th-century paintings by Blechen, Gäertner and Schinkel himself. There are refreshment facilities at the palace but some visitors might prefer the cool surroundings of the Café Eosander across the road.

Charlottenburg, Luisenplatz. Tel: 320911.
Open: Tuesday to Sunday 10am–5pm.
Admission charge. U-Bahn to Richard-Wagner-Platz. Buses 109, 110, 121, 145.

The Liberty Bell in Schöneberg Town Hall, where President Kennedy made his famous speech

SCHÖNEBERG

The medieval village of Sconenberch received its charter in 1264 and remained independent from Berlin until the great municipal shake-up of 1920. By that time it was already a desirable residential suburb, thanks to the land speculators who moved in after the Wars of Unification. By the 1920s the character of Schöneberg had changed. The area around Nollendorfplatz had become a centre of gay life, as the English novelist Christopher Isherwood famously testifies in his Berlin novels *Mr Norris Changes Trains* and *Goodbye to All That* (on which the film *Cabaret* is based). Isherwood himself lived 'the life of the unemployed' at 17 Nollendorf-strasse from March 1929 until February 1933 and paints a generally unflattering picture of Schöneberg: '...street leading into street of houses like shabby monumental safes crammed with the tarnished valuables and second-hand furniture of a bankrupt middle class'. Isherwood also captures the sense of foreboding many Berliners felt in those troubled times.

When the Nazis came to power, the character of the area changed once again. The nightclubs were closed down and homosexuals and other 'deviants' persecuted, while the Sportspalast on Pallas Strasse (no longer standing) became one of Hitler's favourite venues for speechmaking. (Much of the surviving newsreel footage of the dictator was filmed here.) During World War II the Kammergericht (Supreme Court of Justice) on the northwestern edge of Kleist Park was the venue for infamous show trials, including that of the conspirators of the July plot against Hitler's life. The presiding judge, Roland Freisler, was killed when the building was destroyed during an Allied bombing raid in 1945.

Schöneberg's town hall (Rathaus Schöneberg), on Martin-Luther Strasse, was home to West Berlin's municipal government from 1948 to 1989; it was from this balcony that US President John F Kennedy made his famous '*Ich bin ein Berliner*' speech before half a million people on 26 June 1963.
U-Bahn to Nollendorfplatz.

SIEGESSÄULE (Victory Column)

The location of this monument on Grosser Stern, a radial point of five avenues surrounded by the Tiergarten, seems so ideal that it comes as a surprise to learn that it was moved here by Hitler in 1938 from its original position on the square in front of the Reichstag. He intended it to be the focal point of Nazi parades along the Strasse des 17 Juni, then known as the East-West Axis.

The Victory Column was erected in 1873 to commemorate Prussian success in the Wars of Unification against, successively, Denmark, Austria and France. Reliefs showing military exploits of the era decorate the inner walls, and the fluted sandstone column, 67m high and built on a colonnaded pedestal of red granite, is ornamented with captured cannon. The oversized statue of Victory which crowns the summit weighs 35 tonnes and is known to Berliners as 'Gold Else'.

Approach the entrance from the subway on Strasse des 17 Juni and it is possible to climb the 285 steps to the viewing platform, with splendid views across the Tiergarten towards the Reichstag and the Brandenburg Gate – ideal for photographs.
Tiergarten, Grosser Stern. Tel: 3912961. Open: Monday 1–6pm, Tuesday to Sunday 9am–6pm. Admission charge. U-Bahn to Hansaplatz. S–Bahn to Bellevue. Bus 100 to Grosser Stern.

'Gold Else' on the Victory Column presides over the Tiergarten

SPANDAU

Situated about 12km northwest of Berlin centre, Spandau, founded in 1232, is the city's oldest suburb. Its site, at the confluence of the rivers Havel and Spree, made it an ideal trading post and an important strategic point, which is why Spandau has had a castle since the 13th century. In more recent times Spandau was famous as the place of incarceration of Hitler's deputy, Rudolf Hess. Hess was sentenced to life imprisonment by the Nuremberg Tribunal and served a total of 41 years, more than 20 of them as the gaol's sole prisoner. Despite a public outcry, the Soviet government refused to release him and he committed suicide in 1987 at the age of 93. (While Spandau itself was in the Western sector, the gaol was administered jointly by all four Allied powers, including the Soviet Union.) The prison was immediately flattened and the site became a supermarket for the British forces stationed there.

The Zitadelle (Citadel), like the old town itself, is situated on an island and

Zitadelle – Strasse am Juliusturm 1/20. Open: Tuesday to Friday 9am–5pm, Saturday and Sunday 10am–5pm. Admission charge. U-Bahn to Zitadelle Bahnhof.
Gotisches Haus – Breite Strasse 32. Open: Tuesday to Friday 10am–5pm, Saturday and Sunday 10am–1pm. Free.

its red brick fortifications, surrounded by a moat, are unmistakeable. The crenellated Julius Tower is the oldest surviving part of the building and dates from about 1200; the core of the remainder is Renaissance, designed by an Italian architect for the Elector Joachim II of Brandenburg in 1557. Inside the cobbled courtyard is a statue of Berlin's founder, Albert the Bear. Immediately to his right are the ruins of

Spandau's island citadel, reminder of an independent past

the old arsenal, destroyed by Napoleon in 1813. The Old Magazine dates from 1580 but the bastions and the new arsenal are 19th-century. Cannon were manufactured in a foundry near Spandau in the 1850s. In 1860 a brand new model was sent on an 11,000km journey to the Russian settlement of Khabarovsk in the Far East. It languished there for more than a century but has recently been returned, the journey paid for by local businessmen.

Despite wartime bombing the half-timbered houses and cottages of the Altstadt (Old Town) have been well preserved. The Gotisches Haus at 32 Breite Strasse is Berlin's oldest building, now the town museum. Outside the sturdy, 15th-century Nikolaikirche in Reformationsplatz is a monument to the Reformation, erected in 1889 to commemorate the introduction of Protestantism to Mark Brandenburg. The picturesque area to the northeast, known as the Kolk, boasts a lock, quaint old houses and remains of the town wall. *U-Bahn to Altstadt-Spandau.*

TEMPELHOF

Nowadays Tempelhof is a conventional civilian airport carrying passengers to and from various destinations in Germany and Western Europe, yet it still has a distinctive atmosphere. There are no motorway approaches because it is in the heart of the city. There are hardly any signposts and the terminal itself is hidden from view.

In 1948, at the height of the Cold War, things were very different. On 23 June the Soviet authorities abruptly announced that all road and rail routes to and from West Berlin were closed 'because of technical problems'. This disingenuous message signalled the start

Memorial commemorating the Berlin airlift at Templehof

of an 11-month blockade, an attempt to starve the population of West Berlin into surrender and to force the Allies out of the city. The first instinct of the US military governor, General Lucius Clay, was to prise open the land route by confronting the Communists head-on, but it was eventually decided to supply the beleaguered citizens by air, mainly from the US airbase at Tempelhof. From 26 June 1948 to 12 May 1949 US Dakota C-47 transport planes and specially converted British Lancasters and flying boats made a total of 300,000 flights and managed to drop more than 1.8 million tonnes of supplies – food, fuel and medicine – over the western zones of the city. More than 70 lives were lost but the Soviets surrendered and the blockade was lifted. A memorial outside the airport commemorates the event. *U-Bahn to Platz der Luftbrücke.*

TOPOGRAPHIE DES TERRORS

A large prefabricated hut stands on the site of the School of Industrial Arts and Crafts; from May 1933 this was the headquarters of the Gestapo (State Secret Police) and Prinz-Albrecht Strasse 8 soon became 'the most feared address in Berlin'. Those arrested were driven through the twin brick pillars of the garden gate (still standing) and into the basement to await interrogation and torture. The flattened-out area beneath a canopy to the side of the hut marks the site of the cell block where prisoners were held for months, sometimes years, before being moved on to the larger gaols and concentration camps of the Third Reich. The SS also owned the next-door building (formerly a hotel) and the imposing Prinz-Albrecht Palais which fronted on to Wilhelmstrasse. On these premises the worst of the war crimes perpetrated by the Nazi regime were conceived, organised and overseen by Heinrich Himmler's evil legionaries, including Reynhard Heidrich, Ernst Kaltenbrunner and Adolf Eichmann.

The exhibition hall is built over the foundations of an annexe to Gestapo headquarters, containing a kitchen and canteen built by prisoners from Sachsenhausen concentration camp between 1943 and 1944. Inside is photographic documentation charting the history of the buildings which once occupied the site, the rise and expansion of the Nazi state, the consequences of its racist and expansionist policies, the fate of its opponents and the career of its leading executives.

Outside, a wooden flight of steps leads to a viewing platform which looks out over the area, known during the War as the Regierungsviertel (Government Quarter). The future of the site is still a subject of controversy. There are those who believe it is time to bury the past and use this prime site for urban redevelopment. Others argue that the darker pages of Germany's past must be confronted, and it was this view that prompted the organisation of the Topographie des Terrors exhibition in 1987 (Berlin's 750th anniversary). Plans for a more permanent memorial have still to be finalised.

Kreuzberg, Stresemannstrasse 110. Tel: 25486703. Open: daily 10am–6pm. Free. U- or S-Bahn to Anhalter Bahnhof.

UNTER DEN LINDEN

This 1.6km-long avenue (see pages 98–9), running from the Brandenburg Gate to Museumsinsel, became the incongruous heart of East Berlin when the city was divided after World War II. Incongruous, because Unter den Linden ('Under the Limes') had been the symbol of Prussian imperialism for hundreds of years, and had become, during the 18th and 19th centuries, the setting for a string of grandiose neo-classical buildings, including cathedrals, palaces, museums and embassies.

Originally a route for royal hunting parties heading for the Tiergarten woods, Unter den Linden was laid out in 1648 by Elector Friedrich Wilhelm, who had the first lime trees planted along its length. The avenue's role as an imperial showpiece was developed in the 18th century, with the erection of the Deutsche Staatsoper, St Hedwigs Kathedral (see page 84), both designed by Knobelsdorff for Frederick the Great, and the Alte Königliche Bibliothek (Old Royal Library), all of which were set around a square known as the Forum Fridericianum, now called Bebelplatz (see page 99). The theme of imperial

The hated Topography of Terror Museum (above and right), site of the headquarters of the Gestapo (State Secret Police)

pomp was continued in the 19th and early 20th centuries with the addition of Schinkel's Neue Wache, the palace guardhouse, built in 1818 to resemble a Roman temple (see page 80), and the Protestant Cathedral, the Berliner Dom, which opened in 1905 at the lower end of the avenue (see page 30).

Communist rule brought many changes to Unter den Linden, already ravaged by Allied air raids. The Kaiser's palace was demolished and eventually replaced with Erich Honecker's modern Palast der Republik in 1973; the equestrian statue of Frederick the Great was removed from its site outside the Humboldt University in 1950, to be returned in the 1980s; modern blocks were hurriedly built to fill bomb sites; names of streets and functions of buildings were changed. During the same era, monuments were raised to victims of Fascism and the lime trees that had been cut down by Hitler to make room for Nazi processions were replanted. After the Berlin Wall had come down, Unter den Linden resumed its role as a focus for a unified city; its future development is sure to reflect the new aspirations and problems of Berlin.

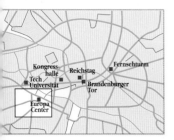

Around Ku'damm

This walk explores Berlin's exciting West End and shopping centre. *Allow about 1½ to 2 hours.*

Start at Bahnhof Zoologischer Garten. Leave the station by the Hardenbergplatz exit.

1 BAHNHOF ZOOLOGISCHER GARTEN

After dark, Zoo station is the haunt of the city's youth on the way to a night out; by day it's a busy transit point for commuters and back-packers. Once you arrive here you know you are in the heart of modern Berlin and the excitement is infectious, the pace frenetic. Across the road is the neo-Romanesque Kaiser Wilhelm Gedächtniskirche (Memorial Church – see page 59) and Breitscheidplatz, where anything goes, from busking and fund-raising stunts to street fairs and rock concerts.

Cross over into Joachimstaler Strasse, pass the Kaiser Wilhelm Gedächtniskirche (Memorial Church), and turn left into Tauentzienstrasse. Continue past the Europa-Center and the KaDeWe department store to Wittenbergplatz.

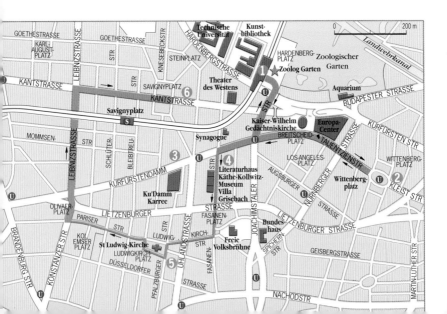

Shoppers take a break on the Ku'damm

2 WITTENBERGPLATZ

This neo-classical station has a remarkable 1920s art deco interior with a large, hangar-like booking hall and wooden ticket office. Most striking, however, are the colourful period posters advertising Opel cars, the German Automobile Club, Bechstein pianos, Cafe Möhring and the city's electric tramways. *Return along the same route to Kurfürstendamm.*

3 KURFÜRSTENDAMM

Flushed with victory over the French in 1871, the Chancellor of the newly united Germany, Otto von Bismarck, planned a grand avenue, on the lines of the Champs Elysées in Paris, to run westwards from the Tiergarten. The building boom which followed led speculators to develop a new West End, encompassing the former villages of Schöneberg, Wilmersdorf and Charlottenburg. These suburbs became the nest of the *nouveaux riches* and of the professional classes. Not long afterwards the Ku'damm began to rival Friedrichstrasse as a centre of Berlin nightlife. Following World War II, US investment, dictated by the exigencies of the Cold War, led to the rebuilding of the devastated avenue as a capitalist showcase and a goad to East Berlin. Although it has lost some of its gloss, the Ku'damm remains a paradise for shoppers, with wide, tree-shrouded pavements, a diverting café scene and plenty of public transport. *Turn left into Fasanenstrasse.*

4 FASANENSTRASSE

The handsome mansions in this street date from the 1890s. Of particular interest is no 23, the Literaturhaus, which has a bookshop in the basement (Kohlhaas und Co), a cultural centre and an art gallery with a delightful garden café, the Wintergarten. Next door is the Käthe-Kollwitz-Museum (see page 60). At no 25 is another Jugendstil villa, the Villa Grisebach, built between 1891 and 1895 by Hans Grisebach and now a private art gallery. *At Fasanenplatz, turn right into Ludwigkirchstrasse.*

5 LUDWIGKIRCHPLATZ

Pleasantly secluded gardens, in front of the church, make an ideal place for resting the feet and sorting out one's impressions. A quietly splashing fountain calms frayed nerves and there is a children's playground to divert the youngsters. *Turn right into Pariser Strasse, skirting Olivaer Platz. Cross the Ku'damm into Leibnizstrasse. After the railway bridge, turn right into Kantstrasse, which leads into Savignyplatz.*

6 SAVIGNYPLATZ

Bars, nightclubs and restaurants cluster round this bustling square, which resounds to the rumble of the S-Bahn overhead. Savignyplatz is the place to start an evening at the heart of Berlin's nightlife, with its inexhaustable supply of restaurants, bars and clubs. No 5, on the northern side of the square, was the home of the satirical artist, Georg Grosz, after he returned from exile in the US at the end of the War.

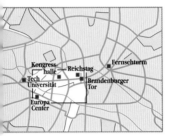

Tiergarten

This walk takes you through Berlin's most famous park and away from the rush and bustle of the city. *Allow 2 hours.*

Begin from Tiergarten S-Bahn station.

1 TIERGARTEN

Literally the Animal Garden, this park was once a royal forest stocked with wild boar and deer for the hunt. In 1745 Frederick the Great commissioned G N Knobelsdorff to enhance the land with statues and paths, but it was not until the 1830s that Peter Joseph Lenné redesigned the 212-hectare park to give it its present appearance. At the end of World War II the few blasted trees that remained were chopped down by cold and starving Berliners and the land was converted into allotments. In 1949 the mayor of West Berlin, Ernst Reuter, began the park's renaissance by ceremonially planting the first tree. Today it is once again the Berliners' favourite park, a place to stroll, to walk the dog and to picnic.
On your right is the Berlin-Pavillon.

2 BERLIN-PAVILLON

The Berlin-Pavillon houses a permanent architectural exhibition of plans for the future development of Berlin.

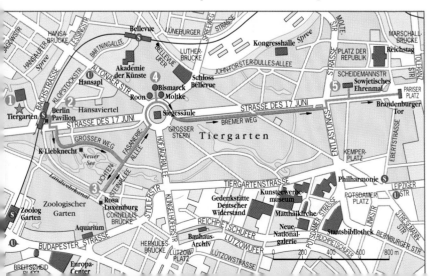

Berlin-Pavillon – open: Tuesday to Sunday 10am–8pm. Closed: Monday. Admission charge.

Cross Strasse des 17 Juni and follow the path Grosser Weg. To the right of the pathway is the Karl Liebknecht memorial. Turn right at the end of Grosser Weg into Lichtensteinallee and follow to canal bridge, where a bronze plaque commemorates Rosa Luxemburg.

3 MEMORIALS TO KARL LIEBKNECHT AND ROSA LUXEMBURG

The radical socialist Karl Liebknecht founded the Spartakusbund (Spartacus League) in 1916 as an alternative to the Social Democratic Party. In the chaotic aftermath of World War I, while workers and revolutionaries engaged in street fighting with soldiers returning from the front, Liebknecht and his Polish comrade-in-arms, Rosa Luxemburg, were planning a Communist uprising. It was immediately put down by the government. In January 1919 the two were forced out of hiding by fanatical members of the right wing Free Corps, interrogated, beaten and murdered; their bodies were subsequently discovered in the Landwehrkanal.

Return along Lichtensteinallee and continue along Fasanerieallee as far as Grosser Stern. Cross the roundabout, passing the Siegessäule (Victory Column). Take the footpath through the trees to the Bismarck monument.

4 MONUMENTS TO BISMARCK, MOLTKE AND ROON

The three heroes of the Franco-Prussian War – two generals and the future unifier of Germany – are commemorated in statuary of varying degrees of pretention. The Bismarck monument was originally positioned close to the Reichstag and was moved to its present site by Hitler in 1938.

From the Bismarck monument cross Strasse des 17 Juni and take the Bremer Weg. The second path on the right leads through the Rosengarten. Take the path in a easterly direction through the Tiergarten to the Entlastungs-Strasse. Rejoin the Strasse des 17 Juni. On the left is the Soviet memorial.

The statue of Otto von Bismarck, the 'Iron Chancellor', in the Tiergarten

5 SOWJETISCHES EHRENMAL

A grandiose monument in Socialist Realist style, using marble from the ruins of Hitler's Chancellery, this memorial commemorates the 20,000 soldiers of the Red Army who perished in the battle for Berlin in uncompromising terms. The Russian inscription reads: 'Eternal glory to the fallen heroes in battle with the German Fascist aggressor for the freedom and independence of the Soviet Union.' Two Soviet T-34 tanks stand on mute guard at the entrance to the garden.

Pass through the Brandenburger Tor to Pariser Platz.

Unter den Linden

This stroll takes you through the historic centre of Berlin. *Allow 1½ hours.*

Begin at Unter den Linden S-Bahn station.

1 UNTER DEN LINDEN

At one time this was the heart of Imperial Berlin, where Prussian soldiers paraded, bands played and crowds promenaded, and where tourists flocked to admire the succession of architectural set pieces by Knobelsdorff, Schinkel and others which adorned the lower end of the avenue (see Berliner Dom, page 30 and also pages 92–3). Most of these were destroyed during World War II but have since been restored.

By way of contrast, the top end of the avenue remains an unhappy aggregate of building sites, little-patronised modish shops and relics of a bygone era – the offices of Intourist, Aeroflot and the former Soviet, now Russian Embassy. The four rows of lime trees from which the avenue takes its name are still here, but its original purpose as a processional route leading from the Schloss to the Brandenburger Tor (Brandenburg Gate) has been lost.

Continue as far as Charlottenstrasse. Turn right, cross Französische Strasse, then turn left into Gendarmenmarkt (see page 56).

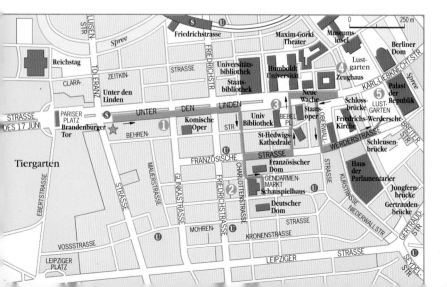

2 SCHAUSPIELHAUS (Playhouse)

This fine neo-classical building (see page 56) is by Schinkel and was erected between 1818 and 1821. The statues and sculptures decorating its exterior, including the sun chariot ridden by Apollo, were executed by Rauch and Christian Friedrich Tieck to designs by Schinkel, who specified every detail of the building down to the shape of the door handles. The auditorium is now a concert hall. Outside the theatre is a towering marble figure of Friedrich Schiller (1759–1805), most famous as the writer of *Ode to Joy*, the text of Beethoven's Choral Symphony.
Return to Französische Strasse and turn right, then left into Bebelplatz.

3 BEBELPLATZ

Formerly Opernplatz, the square now takes its name from August Bebel, leader of the German Social Democratic party before World War I. It was designed as part of the Forum Fredericianum, Frederick the Great's tribute to himself and to the grandeur of ancient Rome, which he intended Berlin to emulate. The city's first theatre, the neo-classical Deutsche Staatsoper, stands in the centre of the square. Mendelssohn, Liszt, Richard Strauss and the great conductor Wilhelm Furtwängler all gave performances here. On 10 May 1933, the Nazi propaganda chief, Joseph Goebbels, orchestrated a public book-burning on the square, consigning the works of many eminent authors, including Sigmund Freud, Karl Marx and Thomas Mann, to the flames for being 'un-

> **Zeughaus** – open: Thursday to Tuesday 10am–6pm. Admission charge for temporary exhibitions.

German in spirit'. At the western end of the square is the Universitäts-bibliothek (University Library), built from 1775 to 1780 by Georg Unger and known as the 'kommode' because of its supposed resemblance to a chest of drawers.
Leave Bebelplatz and cross Unter den Linden to the Zeughaus.

4 ZEUGHAUS (Arsenal)

Now the German History Museum, this is Berlin's first and arguably most distinguished baroque palace, designed by Johann Nering in 1695. The inner courtyard, the Schlüterhof, is named after Andreas Schlüter, who sculpted the masks of dying warriors on the walls.
Cross over into Oberwallstrasse, then left into Werderstrasse, passing Friedrichs-werdersche-Kirche. Cross Schleusen Brücke into Lustgarten.

5 LUSTGARTEN

The Royal Palace, the Stadtschloss, once occupied this site and there has been a proposal to resurrect it. More recently, the square was the headquarters of the East German government; you can still see the white former Foreign Ministry and the gigantic Palast der Republik (1973–6), intended as a lasting monument to socialism but now destined for the scrapheap.

Masks of dying warriors line the walls of the Zeughaus

THE WALL: STORY OF A COMMUNITY

One day in August 1961 the residents of Bernauer Strasse woke up to find armed policemen hastily laying rows of barbed wire immediately outside their front doors. There was no room in this densely built-up neighbourhood of Prenzlauerberg for a wall or even a fence, so the houses themselves became a makeshift barrier between East and West. As the implications of what was happening began to dawn on the bewildered inhabitants, their first thought was of escape. Leaving by the front door or ground floor windows quickly became impossible when the authorities ordered all exits facing the street to be bricked up. In desperation men, women and children began leaping from upper storey windows. Firemen on the western side tried to break their fall, but 20 people died, some under a hail of bullets. The remaining residents of Bernauer Strasse were trapped in the East, powerless to do anything except wave forlornly to their loved ones from the tops of their step-ladders.

Escape from the bricked-up houses was no longer an option; other ways had to be found. In 1964 more than 30 people made their way to freedom through a tiny, unlit tunnel in the cellar of a bakery. To prevent a recurrence the authorities demolished much of the street to make way for a fortification 100m wide, patrolled by guards and dogs and overlooked by watch-towers. The final symbol of hope – the Church of the Reconciliation – was left stranded in the death strip.

The fate of Bernauer Strasse and its inhabitants finds echoes in the experience of all Berliners, so it is fitting that it was residents of that street who, at 9.15 on the evening of 9 November 1989, became the first East Berliners to cross freely to the West in more than 28 years. Today remnants of the wall are still clearly visible along the hill that is still called Bernauer Strasse. Here and there a luxuriant overgrowth of weeds and long grass gives way to barren stretches of

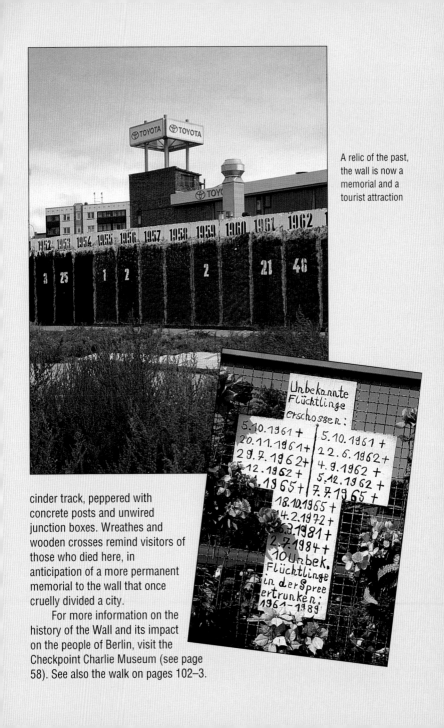

A relic of the past, the wall is now a memorial and a tourist attraction

1952 1953 1954 1955 1956 1957 1958 1959 1960 1961 1962

3 25 1 2 2 21 46

Unbekannte
Flüchtlinge
erschossen:

5.10.1961 +   5.10.1961 +
20.11.1961 +   22.6.1962 +
29.7.1962 +   4.9.1962 +
12.1962 +   5.12.1962 +
.1965 +   7.7.1965 +
18.10.1965 +
14.2.1972 +
.3.1981 +
2.7.1984 +
10 unbek.
Flüchtlinge
in der Spree
ertrunken:
1961-1989

cinder track, peppered with concrete posts and unwired junction boxes. Wreathes and wooden crosses remind visitors of those who died here, in anticipation of a more permanent memorial to the wall that once cruelly divided a city.

For more information on the history of the Wall and its impact on the people of Berlin, visit the Checkpoint Charlie Museum (see page 58). See also the walk on pages 102–3.

The Wall

This walk follows part of the route of the former Berlin Wall. *Allow 3 hours.*

Start at Kochstrasse U-Bahn and walk north into Friedrichstrasse.

1 HAUS AM CHECKPOINT CHARLIE

Alpha, Bravo, Charlie... Of all the border posts only Charlie, located at that most sensitive of spots, the Friedrichstrasse, captured the popular imagination. Here, in October 1961, US and Soviet tanks confronted one another in a dangerous game of 'call my bluff' while the politicians wrangled over the issue of Allied military access to East Berlin. On 22 June 1990, Charlie, now surplus to requirements, was finally hoisted away by crane, to the accompaniment of brass bands and a military parade, the last by the joint occupying powers.

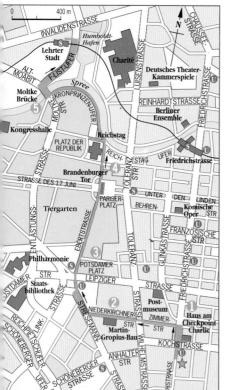

Turn left into Zimmerstrasse, where you will see a wooden cross marking the grave of 18-year-old Peter Fechter, who bled to death while trying to escape over the Wall in 1962.

2 NIEDERKIRCHNERSTRASSE

It is already becoming difficult to appreciate how formidable the Wall was at the height of its monstrous development. Behind the front line concrete barrier, covered with smooth piping to make gripping difficult, was the death strip, a 100m-wide zone of ancillary fences, guard dog tracks, anti-vehicle trenches, alarms and observation towers. Few managed to survive this murderous obstacle course.

Leave Niederkirchnerstrasse and follow Stresemannstrasse to Potsdamer Platz.

3 POTSDAMER PLATZ

When the Wall went up this once famous square was condemned to

WALL STATISTICS
Length 166km
Height 4m
295 watchtowers
43 bunkers
262 dog runs
14,000 border guards
80 fatalities, including 25 guards

remain a desolate wasteland. It had become a no-go area; redevelopment was impossible and, although under-ground trains passed from East to West, they failed to stop at Potsdamer Platz station, which remained sealed up. Now the station has reopened and the new offices of Daimler-Benz will occupy perhaps half of the site. The future of the rest of Potsdamer Platz has still to be decided.
Walk up Ebertstrasse to the Brandenburger Tor.

4 FROM THE BRANDENBURGER TOR TO THE REICHSTAG
The Wall ran directly in front of the Gate before skirting the rear of the Reichstag. During the Cold War, Western politicians made a point of coming to this spot to draw attention to the significance of this most famous East–West divide. When reports came in of a relaxation of the border restrictions on 9 November 1989, it was to this point that the crowd headed for celebration. At the northeastern corner of the Reichstag building, near the river, is a modest line of inscribed white crosses, the 'Memorial to the Victims of War and Violence'.
Follow the Reichstag-Ufer, then the Kronprinzen-Ufer westwards to the Moltke Brücke (bridge).

The site of Checkpoint Charlie

5 RIVER CROSSINGS
The border between East and West ran across the Spree a little way downstream from the ornate sandstone Moltke bridge (see page 36), named after the victorious general of the Wars of Unification. (Note the bellicose cherubs sporting martial gear.) Berlin's waterways were a favourite means of escape in the early days of the Wall's history but not all attempts were successful – the first death was recorded in August 1961, when Gunter Litfin was shot by East German border guards while trying to swim across the Teltow canal. Immediately barriers and booby traps were lowered into the water to deter others, while patrol boats monitored the entire network. This did not prevent the crew of a passenger steamer from hijacking their own ship and navigating it safely to the Western bank, after getting the captain drunk and locking him in his cabin.

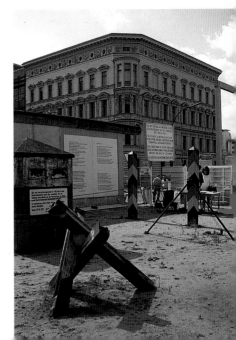

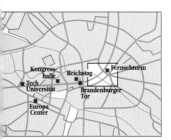

Nikolai Quarter

This walk takes you through the heart of the old centre of Berlin. *Allow 1 hour.*

Start at Alexanderplatz station. Walk southwest through Alexanderplatz. Cross Spandauer Strasse and enter the square opposite.

1 'MARX-ENGELS FORUM'/FORUM AN DER RATHAUSSTRASSE

At the time of writing two massive, monolithic bronze statues of the famous Socialist prophets occupy central position in this otherwise unremarkable expanse, which is a park only in the minds of the planners. After the Wall had come down, someone spray-painted the following 'apology' on to the plinth: 'It's not our fault, we're sorry – maybe next time things will turn out better.'
Return to Spandauer Strasse and turn right into Am Nussbaum.

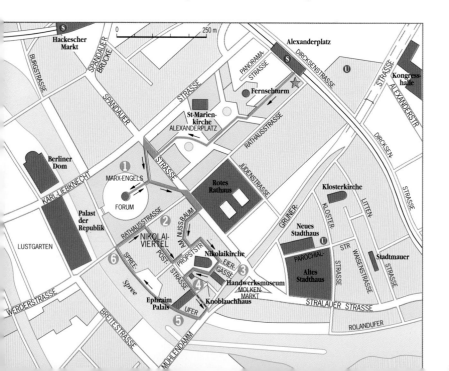

2 NIKOLAIVIERTEL (The Nikolai Quarter)

In the 1980s the East German authorities finally got around to re-creating this historic quarter of the city, once the heart of the twinned settlements of Berlin-Cölln. Most of the original buildings, including the 13th-century church now at the centre of the refashioned 'quarter', were reduced to rubble during World War II, and the present appearance of the district is only reminiscent of the original.

Nor can one sense the presence of the great literary figures who once drank here, including the playwrights Hauptmann, Ibsen and Strindberg. Nevertheless, with its narrow cobbled streets (mercifully traffic-free) and restored houses, the Nikolai Quarter is a pleasant place to stroll and relax in. Although there is housing here for more than 1,500 people, it is the tourist whose needs are catered for. Pubs and restaurants abound and the prices in the shops put most locals off.

At the end of Am Nussbaum, pass Zum Nussbaum ('At the Nut Tree'), a restored pub whose name honours a 16th-century tavern, once a favourite with the cartoonist, Heinrich Zille. Circle the Nikolaikirche (see page 80) taking in Eiergasse, a street with an old-world flavour and, near by, a restored pub in the manner of the traditional Gaststätte called Zum Paddenwirt.

On the corner of Eiergasse is the Handwerksmuseum.

3 HANDWERKSMUSEUM (Handicraft Museum)

The museum's entrance is on Mühlen-damm. This small but attractive museum is devoted to crafts like printing and woodcarving. Several workshops have been reconstructed along traditional lines.

Turn left from the square in front of the church. On your left is the Knoblauchhaus.

4 KNOBLAUCHHAUS

The house was built by Johann Christian Knoblauch in 1759 and is one of the few buildings to have survived World War II. It is now a museum honouring the family after whom it is named. The Knoblauchs were prominent in Berlin society, supplying the university with a number of professors and the architect of the Neue Synagogue in Oranienburger Strasse. Visitors here included the poet and dramatist Gotthold Ephraim Lessing, who lived round the corner on Nikolaikirchplatz; Moses Mendelssohn, leader of Berlin's Jewish community at the time of Frederick the Great; and the architect Karl Friedrich Schinkel. The Biedermeier room contains period furniture and elsewhere in the house are documents, paintings and drawings.

5 EPHRAIM PALAIS

See page 50.

6 SPREEUFER

The view across the Spree from the café terraces of the Ephraim Palace and Knoblauch House is not picturesque. Move on quickly and the spell cast by the Nikolai Quarter will not be broken!

Turn right into Rathausstrasse and right again into Poststrasse. This brings you back to the central square.

Handwerksmuseum – open: Tuesday to Friday 9am–5pm, Saturday 9am–6pm, Sunday 10am–5pm. Closed: Monday. Admission charge.

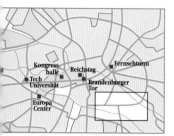

Kreuzberg

This walk explores the heart of one of Berlin's
most cosmopolitan and exciting districts, the
centre of the city's 'alternative' culture and the
home of the Turkish community. *Allow about
1 to 1½ hours.*

Start at Kottbusser Tor U-Bahn station.

1 KOTTBUSSER TOR

Welcome to Kreuzberg! The 'Mountain of the Cross' which
gives the area its name is a small hill in what is now Viktoria
Park. Factories began to overrun the vineyards which once
grew around the slopes of the hill early in the 19th century, and
parts of the district still have an industrial character. During the
revolution of 1848 Kreuzberg was a centre of working class
resistance, of street protests and machine-breaking. The
population was dragooned into the barrack housing known as
Mietskasernen; ever since, Kreuzberg has been one of the most
densely populated of Berlin's districts.

 'Kotti' is typical of radical Kreuzberg where crumbling
19th-century apartment blocks alternate with equally fast-
fading '60s architecture; where *imbiss* stands give the air a
flavour of kebabs and onions; where all-night bars illuminate
the shadows of the U-Bahn girders. The atmosphere is exotic,
suggesting both excess and the unexpected. About a third of
Berlin's 140,000 Turks live in Kreuzberg. Just across the canal
from Kottbusser Tor, on Maybachufer, is the Turkish market,
an outdoor community centre where the locals gather to

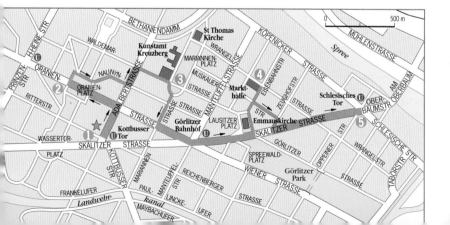

exchange gossip, read Turkish language newspapers and listen to Turkish radio stations. This is also the place to buy fresh figs, dates, spices and peppers.
Walk up Adalbertstrasse. Turn left into Oranienstrasse to Oranienplatz.

2 ORANIENPLATZ
Oranienplatz is in many ways the most attractive part of East Kreuzberg, its sedate gardens surrounded by elegant 19th-century apartments. Oranienstrasse is the main artery and is best explored by hopping on and off the no 129 bus.
Leave Oranienplatz via Naunynstrasse (the house murals are worth looking out for) and Adalbertstrasse, then turn right into Waldemarstrasse. At the square, turn right again into Mariannenstrasse.

3 MARIANNENPLATZ
This is a favourite square with Kreuzbergers, who seem to delight in its slightly worn appearance. It was laid out as a garden by Peter Joseph Lenné (of Tiergarten and Charlottenburg fame) in 1853.

The yellow brick building with its twin pencil-like towers on the west side of the square is the Künstlerhaus Bethanien. It was built as a hospital in the 1840s, avoided demolition in the 1960s and has recently been converted into a first-rate cultural centre with studios, workshops, exhibition and concert rooms and a Turkish bookshop. The Künstlerhaus is the best place to take the cultural pulse of Kreuzberg. On the north side is the Church of St Thomas, which used to stand in the shadow of the Wall. It was completed in 1869 by a pupil of Schinkel's, F Adler. On the south side is a jocular sculpture by D Wolff and G Jendritzko called *Fallen of the Berlin Fire Brigade*, depicting

a couple of firemen firing water hoses at one another.
Turn left on to Oranienstrasse and continue along Skalitzer Strasse. Turn left along the eastern side of Lausiter Platz and right into Eisenbahn-Strasse.

Kreuzberg's run-down appearance is grist to the mill of the alternative culture

4 MARKTHALLE
This colourful market caters for the locals, selling vegetables, cheese and fruit.
Continue along Skalitzer Strasse to Schlesisches Tor U-Bahn.

5 SCHLESISCHES TOR
The square which occupies the site of the old Silesian Gate now marks the eastern frontier of Kreuzberg. Architectural buffs will enjoy the Jugendstil station which dates from 1902 and was one of the original stations on the first U-Bahn line, known today as the Orient Express.

Prenzlauer Berg

This walk explores Berlin's most famous old working-class district, now becoming a favourite night haunt with its restaurants, cafés and bars. *Allow 2 hours.*

Start at Schönhauser Allee U-Bahn station.

1 SCHÖNHAUSER ALLEE

A good spot to sample Prenzlauer Berg's new, up-market image. Neglected after the War, this district gained a reputation in the '60s and '70s for gritty radical opposition to the GDR. As the fabric of its buildings continued to crumble and the squatters moved in, it also attracted gangs of skinheads and

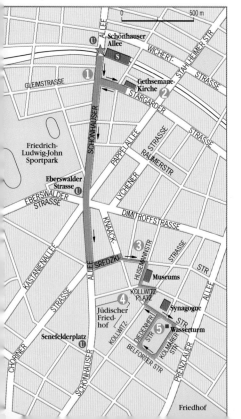

malcontents. Attempts to renovate the area were already in progress before the Wall came down but the process of rejuvenation has accelerated – not all the locals are happy with the result.

Around the station gather a string of pizzerias, plush bars, smart restaurants, fashion boutiques and jewellers – all almost disturbingly new and with a slight air of not belonging.

Head down Schönhauser Allee and turn first left into Stargarder Strasse. On your left is the Gethsemane Kirche.

2 GETHSEMANE KIRCHE
(Gethsemane Church)

The modest appearance of the plain red brick church with the green spire belies its dramatic recent history. During the last days of the Honecker regime in the autumn of 1989 the Gethsemane Kirche became the unofficial headquarters of the democracy movement known as Neues Forum (New Forum). Hopeful faces lit by candlelight during nightly vigils for peace left an enduring impression on visitors, including representatives of the world's media.

Continue down Schönhauser Allee, past the

junction with Eberswalder Strasse, then turn left into Sredzkistrasse. On the corner are the former premises of Schultheiss' brewery, dating from 1891, now an off-beat 'cultural centre' known as the Franz-Club. Turn right into Husemannstrasse.

3 HUSEMANNSTRASSE

With its windmills and open rolling fields, Prenzlauer Berg was once Berlin's bread basket. All this changed with the coming of industry in the 19th century, as a result of which the district acquired the unenviable reputation of having the largest population density per building in the world. Workers were packed like sardines into *Mietskasernen*, vast, six-storey lodging houses whose once elegant façades hid a grim succession of cramped and gloomy back courtyards. To gain some impression of what life was like here, visit the Museum of Berlin Working Class Life around 1900 at no 12 (see page 70). The renovation of Husemannstrasse began in the 1980s and is almost complete. It marks the beginning of a revitalised café life with a trendy, up-market

Artist Käthe Kollwitz, chronicler of working-class Prenzlauer Berg

feel not popular with all the locals.

4 KOLLWITZPLATZ

The square is named after the artist Käthe Kollwitz (1861–1945), who lived near by in a house since demolished. Children play unselfconsciously around her statue in the middle of the square which is how she would have liked it. A favourite local night spot is Restauration 1900, a rather chic café-restaurant with outside tables and good but pricey food and drink. *Turn left on to Knaackstrasse. On your right is a garden.*

5 WASSERTURM (Water Tower)

Now converted into apartments, the polygonal tower was opened as a sanitary measure in 1877. The Nazis found a more sinister use for it – it became a prison for torturing and murdering Social Democrat and Communists, who offered strong resistance in Prenzlauer Berg. *Return to Kollwitzplatz. The nearest station is Senefelderplatz. Note the squat near the entrance.*

Sachsenhausen

This walk, more in the manner of a pilgrimage, takes in one of the most notorious of the Nazi concentration camps. *Allow 3 hours.*

Start at Oranienburg S-Bahn station. Turn right into Stalsunder Steg, then into Bernauerstrasse. Turn left into Strasse der Einheit and right into Strasse der Nationen. Just past the entrance to the grounds is a small bookshop and information centre.

SACHSENHAUSEN CONCENTRATION CAMP

The concentration camp was opened in July 1936 at the same time as Berlin was hosting the Olympic Games. By the end of World War II about half of the 220,000 prisoners who had passed through the gates had been murdered or had died from illness and neglect. The victims included political opponents, Jews, Soviet POWs, homosexuals, gypsies, criminals and other 'anti-social elements'. Sachsenhausen was also a training school for camp commanders and the headquarters of the Concentration Camp Inspectorate. In 1945 the Soviet military police took over Sachsenhausen as an internment camp for their own prisoners – an estimated 20,000 of them perished.

The future of Sachsenhausen is a highly sensitive issue. Some, notably the Jewish community, want the memorial to

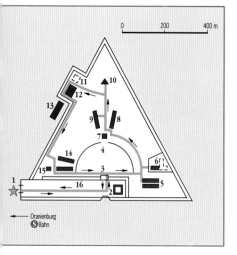

SITE PLAN
1 Entrance
2 International museum
3 Tower 'A'
4 Appellplatz
5 Restored barracks
6 Underground cells and prison
7 Site of gallows
8 Camp Museum (formerly kitchen)
9 Cinema (formerly laundry)
10 Memorial
11 Execution ditch
12 Station Z
13 Exhibition hall
14 Infirmary and morgue
15 Pathology department
16 Restored camp wall and electrified fence
Open: April to September 8am–6pm, October to March 9am–4.30pm.
Closed: Monday. Free.

'Work makes Free', the great lie emblazoned over the gate of Sachsenhausen

remain as it is. The local council favours developing part of the site for commercial purposes while preserving its character as a memorial. The most radical plan, by Daniel Libeskind, rejects the museum concept entirely in favour of landscaping the site, with only a nod in the direction of a memorial.

INTERNATIONAL MUSEUM (No 2)

The history of the Jews in Sachsenhausen is told through photographs and artefacts; there is also a section on the forgery and printing press which the Nazis developed here in a vain attempt to subvert the British and US economies.

APPELLPLATZ (Roll Call Square No 4)

The main gate of the camp (3) has the soothing look of a provincial railway station. (The slogan: '*Arbeit macht frei*' means 'Work Makes Free'.) Pass through to the concrete exercise yard, with a view of the watch towers, the perimeter wall and the barbed wire electrified fence. Three times a day the prisoners were herded on to this square in all weathers for roll call and to witness executions on the camp gallows.

CELL-BLOCK (No 6)

This simple white-washed building was once used to detain prisoners of war. Some of the cells have been restored; others, including that belonging to the German resistance leader, Pastor Martin Niemöller, have been converted into shrines with wreaths.

CAMP MUSEUM (No 8)

In the former prison kitchens, this is an exhibition of life in the camp with models and a reconstruction of the tiered bunks on which prisoners had to sleep.

MEMORIAL (No 10)

A simple concrete obelisk carved with inverted triangles, each commemorating one of the 18 categories of prisoner.

STATION Z (No 12)

Only the brick foundations remain of the notorious extermination centre. Soviet prisoners of war were executed here – some 18,000 of them, each believing he was being taken for a 'medical examination'. Behind the wall with the eye chart was an SS soldier who fired a shot into the prisoner's neck through a concealed aperture. The bodies were later disposed of in the adjoining crematorium. Also on the premises was a gas chamber and execution ditch (11).

PATHOLOGY DEPARTMENT (No 15)

Corpses were brought here for dissection and experiment. Gold was removed from teeth and sold, and tattooed skin was made into lampshades or handbags. The cellar in which the bodies were stored can also be visited.

Bus 100

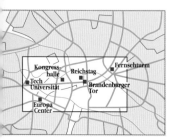

See Berlin's tourist landmarks, East and West, from one of the city's famous double-decker buses – and avoid paying the earth (they leave every 10 minutes). An ideal introduction to the city. See pages 22–3 for route. *Allow about 1 hour.*

Board at Bahnhof Zoologischer Garten.

FROM THE ZOO TO THE TIERGARTEN

The Berlin bus company BVG calls route 100 its 'red thread' from Zoo Station to Alexanderplatz. Before 1989 such a journey from West to East Berlin would have been unthinkable – the Wall would have seen to that. On your left as you travel along busy Budapester Strasse a pair of stone elephants guards the main entrance to Berlin Zoo, while on the right is Berlin's

premier shopping mecca, the Europa-Center (see page 51) – also handy for entertainment and tourist information. The next major port of call is Lützow Platz, which is where to get off for the Bauhaus Archiv, a museum devoted to the famous 1920s school of architecture founded by Walter Gropius (see page 28). The bus now heads north into the Tiergarten, once a hunting ground for the Electors (Tier means animal) and now an attractive park (see pages 96–7 and 132). Directly ahead, at the far end of Hofjäger Allee is one of Berlin's best known monuments, the Siegessäule (Victory Column – see page 89). The golden figure on top is known to Berliners as 'Golden Else'.

FROM THE TIERGARTEN TO THE BRANDENBURGER TOR

The bus continues through the Tiergarten towards the River Spree. The stately building on the left is Schloss

Zoo station is the embarkation point for Bus 100

Bellevue, an 18th-century palace which is also the official residence of the President of the Republic. Also on the left-hand side is the exhibition hall known as the Kongresshalle (see page 60). As the bus passes through Platz der Republik the monumental parliament building, the Reichstag, looms into view (see page 81). As the bus turns right into Friedrich Ebert Strasse it follows the route of the former Berlin Wall. Directly ahead is Berlin's most famous monument, the Brandenburg Gate (see page 34). When the Wall was in place this was the most potent symbol of German division. Nowadays it stands for German unity and hopefully for peace – the original intention when it was conceived in 1788.

THROUGH THE HEART OF IMPERIAL BERLIN

The lime trees which give Unter den Linden its name are still in place but there is no sign now of the military parades that used to pass up and down here in the days of the Kaisers. The first major intersection is Friedrichstrasse, Berlin's red light district before World War I and still a centre of entertainment today. The sequence of majestic architectural set pieces which gave Imperial Berlin its unique character begins on the left with the State Library and the Humboldt University. Next in line is the Neue Wache, or guard house (see page 80), and the Zeughaus (Arsenal), now the Deutsches Historisches Museum (German History Museum). The massive domed building coming up on the left is the Protestant Cathedral commissioned by Kaiser Wilhelm II, who used to wave to the crowds from the balcony of the Royal Palace, which once stood opposite.

Elephants stand guard at the entrance to Berlin's zoo

FROM KARL-LIEBKNECHT-STRASSE TO ALEXANDERPLATZ

To the left of the Cathedral is Museumsinsel (Museum Island – see pages 72–7). The no 100 bus completes its journey by circling Alexanderplatz ('Alex' to locals), once the main square of East Berlin and now ripe for redevelopment. Take the lift to the top of the 362m-high Fernsehturm (TV tower – see page 51) for spectacular views of the city or return to base via the U-Bahn or S-Bahn – both networks have stations on Alexanderplatz.

Boat Trips

In the summer months taking a boat trip is a wonderful way to explore the River Spree and the extensive waterways that flow into it, to the west and to the east of the city.

TOUR 1
FROM TEGEL TO WANNSEE

The Greenwich-Promenade is close to Tegel Park (U-Bahn Tegel). The boat sails across the broad expanses of the Tegeler See before weaving its way through the islands which mark the juncture with the Havel. The first major port of call is Spandau; the magnificent Zitadelle or fort with its 16th-century bastion, the Juliusturm, is clearly visible from the bridge. This is where the Havel and Spree join forces. The boat opts for the narrow neck of the Havel, heading for Freybrücke and the marshy

promontory known as the Tiefwerder. Here the Havel widens again and to the left there are marvellous views of the vast Grunewald Forest as the boat heads towards the smart villas of Kladow. Disembark at Pfaueninsel (Peacock Island) to explore the nature reserve conceived as a love nest for Frederick William II and his mistress, the Countess Lichtenau. Pick up Line 2 at the pier opposite the Island. The boat now passes under the Glienickebrücke linking Berlin and Potsdam, the scene of a number of spy-swops during the Cold War. The next stretch of river takes in Volkspark Klein-Glienicke and Park Babelsberg before navigating the headland at Griebnitzee. The tour finishes several stops further on at

Stern und Kreisschiffahrt GmbH,
Sachtlebenstrasse 60, 14165 Berlin.
Tel: (030) 810 0040.
'Spreefahrt' Horst Duggen,
Geisbergstrasse 28, 10777 Berlin.
Tel: (030) 394 4954.

A cruise on the Havel makes a refreshing change from urban sight-seeing

Wannsee pier, not far from the S-Bahn station.

Stern und Kreisschiffahrt GmbH line 1 leaves from the Greenwich-Promenade in Tegel every day on the hour from 10am to 5pm; line 2 leaves from the Pier near Wannsee station every day on the half hour from 10.30am to 4.30pm. Journey time 6 to 8 hours.

TOUR 2
THE CITY CENTRE

Setting out from the Kongresshalle, the boat heads for the Reichstag building, which looms into view on the right bank. The large tract of scarred wasteland opposite was once part of the Berlin Wall death strip. Beyond the Friedrichstrasse railway bridge is the Museum Island (see pages 72–7). The pretty Nikolai Quarter is on the left as the boat heads for the Mühlendamm lock (see pages 104–5). Several bridges on is the Oberbaumbrücke, where the counter-intelligence chief, Karla, crosses to the west at the climax of John Le Carré's novel *Smiley's People*. The boat now turns into the Landwehrkanal, passing through Kreuzberg (see pages 106–7), the south side of the Tiergarten (see

pages 96–7) and Charlottenburg (see pages 86–7), then back along the Spree to the Kongresshalle (see page 60).

Spreefahrt Horst Duggen Tour I leaves daily from Kongresshalle pier at 9.45am and lasts about 3 hours.

TOUR 3
MÜGGELSEE

This tour's departure point is the Tiergarten pier, from where the boat follows the course of the Spree through the historic Mitte district. The area north of the Jannowitzbrücke is heavily industrialised. Before 1989 this was where the river formed the boundary between East and West, so the neighbouring districts of Friedrichshain on the left bank and Kreuzberg on the right were isolated from one another. The route continues through Treptow to the old town of Köpenick. Just beyond Schlossinsel is the medieval fishermen's quarter of Kietz. Formerly a popular holiday resort with East Berliners, the Grosser Müggelsee remains a natural sanctuary for wildlife (see pages 136–7). *Horst Duggen Spreefahrt Tour II leaves daily from the Tiergarten pier at 1pm and lasts about 4½ hours.*

THE SPREE

Rivers are the lifeblood of all great cities and Berlin is no exception. Slow moving, at times almost torpid, its arteries prone to congealing with mud and silt, the River Spree is on the face of it a surprising source of urban greatness and prosperity. But the Spree has always had one great advantage: it is perfectly situated at the crossroads of major trade routes stretching in every direction – a factor which earned Berlin membership of the most powerful mercantile system of the Middle Ages, the Hanseatic League. With the coming of the Industrial Revolution, human intervention became necessary to adapt the Spree to new demands. Weirs, locks and canals began to appear along every stretch as the river was straightened and diverted to meet the needs of an increasing volume of barge traffic. The Landwehr Canal was completed in 1850, the Spandau Canal in 1859; by the turn of the century additional waterways, like the Teltow and the Hohenzollern, had joined the system. With the canals came the factories and their inevitable by-product, pollution. Once 'somewhat green in colour and clear', the Spree turned murky and sullen. But Berlin

expanded and became wealthy at the river's expense: coal, building materials, iron and steel and petroleum were transported in vast quantities – even today, the Spree carries more goods traffic than the railways.

This is an unassuming river with an almost unique capacity to surprise. What visitor confronting the vista from the Westhafen docks, for example, would suspect that, simply by turning his back, he would encounter the dreamy tree-shrouded stretch which winds its way lazily towards Charlottenburg and the Tiergarten? Today pleasure cruisers ply their trade alongside the barges in ever increasing numbers, but the Spree will never cease to be what it has always been – a working river.

The Spree – a river for all seasons with a charm of its own

Excursions

BRANDENBURG

Some 62km west of Berlin, Brandenburg is the historic capital of the Mark of Brandenburg, a territory once on the frontier of the Holy Roman Empire. Despite wartime bombing, the medieval town is remarkably intact and is currently undergoing extensive restoration. The surrounding countryside is extremely attractive, with beautiful unspoilt woodland and lakes.

Neustadt (New Town)

To avoid the large and frankly ugly industrial suburb, leave the station via Grosse Gartenstrasse then cross the

bridge into Steinstrasse, at the bottom of which is one of two surviving city gates, the Steintortum. Exhibitions are sometimes held here. The large car park in Neustädtische Markt marks the beginning of the New Town, which is built on an island on the River Havel. It was founded in the late 12th century, not long after the 'old' town. On the southern side of the square, hemmed in by '60s apartment blocks, is the Katharinenkirche (St Katherine Church), a red brick building with an ornate tower. The church is 15th-century and there are wall paintings dating from this period behind the high altar, on the ceiling (note the donkey playing the bagpipes) and in the north and south chapels. The Aldermen chapel has a grill decorated with the Brandenburg crest and private pews originally intended for worshipping civic dignitaries. There is also a baroque pulpit, gamely supported by the head of St Paul, dating from 1668.

Town Museum – Frey Haus, Hauptstrasse 96. Tel: 522048. Open: Wednesday to Friday 9am–5pm, Saturday and Sunday 10am–5pm. Closed Monday and Tuesday. Admission charge.

The light and airy interior of the Romanesque cathedral on Dominsel (Cathedral Island)

Tourist Information: Hauptstrasse 51 14776 Brandenburg. Telephone and fax: 23743.
Trains leave from Hauptbahnhof, Friedrichstrasse and Zoologischer Garten.
By road: E51 and E30.

Altstadt (Old Town)

Access to the Old Town is via
Hauptstrasse, which crosses the
omnipresent River Havel. The tram
tracks belie the fact that the area is now
pedestrianised as an incentive to
shoppers. There are coffee bars, pizzerias,
market stalls and tourist information. At
the far end is Altstädtische Markt,
dominated by the late Gothic Rathaus
(town hall), a sturdy brick structure with
a steeped gable. Guarding it is the
Brandenburger Roland, an over-sized
primitive statue which originally stood
outside the Katharinekirche. On
Nikolaiplatz is the other surviving town
gate, in splendid isolation.

Dominsel (Cathedral Island)

Follow Mühlentorstrasse away from the
town hall to Mühlendamm and Cathedral
Island. This is the most attractive part of
town: picturesque, quiet and secluded,
the trees reflected in the calm waters of
the Havel. The island was settled in the
10th century and a Romanesque
cathedral founded shortly afterwards. The
nave, transepts and choir were later raised
and vaulted to create more light and
space. (See the exhibition in the porch.)
The cathedral has an understated beauty;
look out for the former high altar (1375),
now in the south transept and
inexplicably separated from the altar
panels depicting the crucifixion, which
can still be seen in the chancel. The choir
stalls are the work of a master artist, Hans
the wood-carver, and the handsome
Gothic wardrobe for storing vestments is
another fine piece of craftsmanship. The
cathedral organ, dating from 1723 to
1725 and boasting 2,000 pipes, is one of
the best preserved in Germany. On your

Brandenburg's Hauptstrasse in the Old Town

way out, don't miss the Dom café with its
tasty selection of home made *Kuchen*
(cakes) – closed on Mondays.

Also in Brandenburg

Angelika Thielemann's fabric shop and
café on Steinstrasse 21 sells chair
cushions, table-cloths, curtains and
clothing, made using the age-old
technique of printing with woodblocks
then adding indigo dye.

Marienburg Hill (Altstadt) is a park
with fine views of the town, especially
from the look-out tower. There is also an
open-air swimming pool and theatre here.

Lake Beetzsee, near Dominsel, is a
popular venue for regattas. Boat trips are
available to the many lakes, and even as
far as Potsdam and Berlin.

POTSDAM AND SANSSOUCI

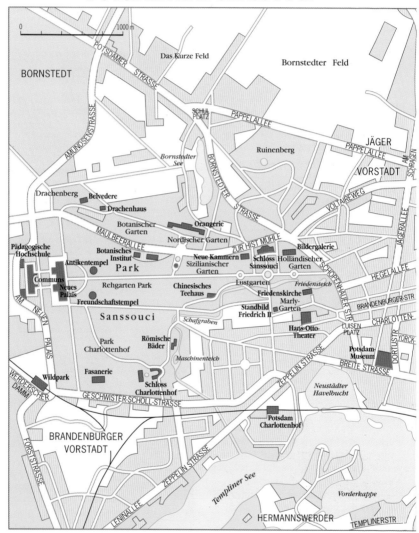

POTSDAM

In 1993 Potsdam celebrated its 1,000th anniversary; its importance, however, dates from the early 18th century, when it became a garrison town and the summer residence of the Hohenzollerns.

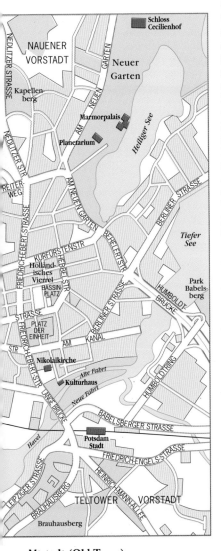

Altstadt (Old Town)

Sadly, many of the buildings which comprised the core of the Old Town, including the Schloss and the Garrison Church, were destroyed during World War II. Among the survivors, to the left of the Lange Brücke, is the elongated, red brick façade of the Marstall, designed by Johann Nering in 1685. Rearing sculptures of horses indicate that this was once the royal stables. Nowadays it is a Filmmuseum (Film Museum). On the opposite side of the bridge is the Nikolaikirche (Nicholas Church). The fortress-like base is the work of Ludwig Persius and dates from the 1830s. Schinkel added the dome 10 years later. A classical portico completes the bizarre ensemble. Much more appealing is the beautifully proportioned Old Town Hall, just to the right, completed in 1753 and now an arts centre (Kulturhaus).

Town Museum – Breite Strasse 13. Tel: 23782. Open: Tuesday to Sunday 9am–5pm. Admission charge.

Film Museum – Marstall Schloss Strasse 1. Tel: 23675. Open: Tuesday to Sunday 10am–5pm. Admission charge.

Nikolaikirche – open: Monday to Saturday 2–5pm, Sunday 11.30am–5pm. Free.

Neustadt (New Town) and Holländisches Viertel (Dutch Quarter)

In 1732 Frederick William II (the Soldier King) ordered the building of a new town running north of Platz der Einheit (Unity Square). Neustadt, the end result, is the most attractive part of Potsdam to have survived.

Tourist Information Office: Friedrich-Ebert-Strasse 5, 0–1561 Potsdam.
Tel: (0331) 23385.
By train: S-Bahn line 3 via Wannsee to Potsdam Stadt.
By road: E51.

Two foreign communities lived in the Neustadt and Holländisches Viertel: the Huguenot presence is recalled by Johann Boumann's French Church dating from 1751, while construction workers from Holland, employed in building the new town, were housed in the aptly named Holländisches Viertel. Several streets of red brick, gabled houses were built to accommodate the Dutch workers, and survive to this day.

The Nauener Tor and the Jägertor, which are situated further to the north are two surviving town gates. The former, with its yellow circular towers, reveals Frederick II's sometimes wayward architectural taste.

Brandenburgerstrasse, with the 'other' Brandenburg Gate set at one end, has now been pedestrianised and is crowded and busy with shoppers. There is an altogether different atmosphere in the quieter, more secluded Lindenstrasse, which has a modest, understated charm.

Schloss Cecilienhof

Bus 695 leaves from outside the Landkreisamt Rathaus and takes the visitor through the Neuer Garten (New Garden), a park laid out after 1786 by Frederick William II. It owes its present appearance to Lenné, who also landscaped the Berlin Tiergarten. Half hidden among the trees are the Marble Palace, the Chinese Shingle House and the Orangery, all of which date from the 18th century.

In total contrast to the park buildings is the Schloss itself, modelled on an English Tudor manor house and commissioned by Kaiser William II shortly before World War I.

Traffic has been outlawed from the centre of Potsdam's New Town

Potsdam's busy Brandenburgerstrasse,
now a pedestrian area

Schloss Cecilienhof is famous for the Potsdam Conference which took place here in 1945. Among the dignitaries attending the conference were the 'big three': Winston Churchill of Great Britain, Harry S Truman of the United States and Joseph Stalin of the Soviet Union. The conference eventually redrew the post-war map of Europe, with profound consequences that are still being felt today.

The rooms in which the delegations met privately, as well as the conference hall itself, may be visited (an English language leaflet tells the story of the conference in more detail).
Neuer Garten. Tel: 9694245. Open: May to October, Tuesday to Sunday 9am–5pm (1st and 3rd Monday of every month 9am–4pm). Admission charge.

SCHLOSS SANSSOUCI

Sanssouci means 'carefree', and it was to escape the burdens of kingship that Frederick the Great built this idyllic summer residence for himself from 1745 to 1747. The architect was his friend, Georg Wenzeslaus von Knobelsdorff, who also designed the new wing of the Charlottenburg Palace (see pages 40–3). Only group tours of the palace apartments are permitted and the demand can be excessive in the summer season, sometimes leading to disappointment.

Sanssouci is a modest, single-storey affair, although the rococo interior is sumptuous, with its marble floors, stuccoed ceilings, richly upholstered furniture, sculptures, precious vases and elegant clocks. Highlights are the study and bedroom of Frederick the Great, the concert chamber and the elliptical Marble Hall with its Corinthian columns of Carrara marble. Of the guest rooms, the fourth, known as the 'Voltaire room' is the most interesting. The great French philosopher is said to have stayed here between 1750 and 1753, while attending Frederick's court as an Ambassador of Enlightenment, but despite helping the king to write a treatise on the ideal ruler, Voltaire became disillusioned with the wilful Prussian monarch, who said of his erstwhile advisor: 'he has the slyness and will of an ape'.

Adjoining the palace is the art gallery. The collection is sadly depleted but there are works by Van Dyck, Rubens and Caravaggio.
Open: daily, tours every 20 minutes, 9am–12.30pm and 1–5pm. Closed: 3rd Monday in the month. Admission charge. Picture Gallery – open: Wednesday to Sunday 9–11.45pm, 12.30–4pm. Admission charge.

Majestic terraces and fountains at Schloss Sanssouci

SCHLOSS SANSSOUCI
The Gardens

The park is one of the most attractive features of the palace. Six terraces lead to the Great Fountain. To the east are the Obelisk Portal, the original entrance to the park, dating from 1748, and the Neptune Grotto (1753). On the other side of Hauptweg is the Friedenskirche (Church of Peace), a mausoleum built by Ludwig Persius for Frederick William IV in 1845 and modelled on an early Christian basilica. Among the figures

adorning the roof of the Chinesisches Teehaus (Chinese Tea House) is a large monkey with the features of Voltaire – Frederick's revenge on his recalcitrant minister! Closer to the Maulbeerallee are the Neue Kammern (New Chambers) of 1771 to 1774 and the Sizilianischer Garten (Sicilian Garden), a Mediterranean fantasy of palm trees, fountains and exotic plants laid out by P J Lenné in 1857.

Conceived in the manner of a Renaissance palace, the stupendous Orangerie dates from 1851 to 1860. Terraces and staircases conspire with the elongated colonnade to overwhelm the visitor. The most famous guests to stay in the lavish guest rooms were Tsar Nicholas I of Russia and his consort, Princess Victoria of England. The Drachenhaus café, a delightful folly in the style of a Chinese pagoda, makes a suitable stopping-off point before returning to the Hauptweg and the New Palace.

Chinesisches Teehaus – open: daily 9am–noon, 12.45–5pm. Closed: 2nd Monday of the month. Admission charge.
Neue Kammern – open: daily 9am–noon, 12.30–5pm. Admission charge.
Orangerie – open: daily 9am–noon, 1–5pm. Admission charge.

Neues Palais (New Palace)

This massive edifice, its three storeys of red brick divided by a series of enormous pilasters surrounded by a balustrade and central cupola, could hardly be more different from Sanssouci. It was constructed between 1763 and 1769 for Frederick the Great by Johann Buring, responsible for the exterior, and Carl von Gontard. Apart from the guest apartments, there are ballrooms, reception rooms and a theatre, while at

The New Palace is an overwhelming baroque presence at Sanssouci

the back of the building is an entire separate accommodation for servants and courtiers known as the Communs. There are group tours of Frederick's apartments, including the music chamber (Frederick was an accomplished flautist), study, dining room and library. At present much of the palace is in a slightly worn state, the result of years of neglect. *Open: Saturday to Thursday 9am–12.45pm, 1.15–5pm. Admission charge. Bus 695 or 606 from Potsdam town.*

The Chinese Tea House

Traditional cottage along the canal in Spreewald, an area of outstanding natural beauty

SPREEWALD

An area of outstanding natural beauty lying about 100km southeast of Berlin, the Spreewald is the perfect antidote to the hectic life of the capital. Slav settlers arrived here in the 7th century and they never regretted it – their successors, the Sorbs, still live here today and speak a language with clear affinities with Polish or Russian. The Romantic poet, Achim von Arnim, visited the Spreewald in 1817 and sang its praises to his wife Bettina. More than 40 years later the novelist, Theodore Fontane, discovered the forests and waterways, likening the latter in his travelogue, *Wanderungen durch die Mark Brandenburg*, to Venice in the days of its infancy. But it was left to the notorious financial speculator, Henry Bethel Strousberg, to make the Spreewald accessible to 19th-century Berliners. Strousberg built a railway line from the Görlitzer Bahnhof to Cottbus, then founded a newspaper to advertise the fact and to recommend the attractions of the region. Today tourists and Berliners alike flock here in their thousands, but as the Spreewald extends for more than 700sq km there should be room for everyone.

The region is comprised of two halves: the Unterspreewald and the Oberspreewald. The scenery is more striking in the Oberspreewald, which extends south of Lübbenau. Here the Spree fragments into dozens of sluggish tributaries, feeding an astonishingly complex network of water channels and canals. The former irrigate the market gardens, which are everywhere, producing onions, gherkins, beetroot and the like, while the latter serve as roads, carrying the produce to market and the local children to school. Boat travel is not the only means of transportation but for

Train from Berlin-Lichterfelde (journey time 1 hour; irregular service).
Severin-Kuhn (Ku'damm 216, tel: 883 1015) offers a coach tour to Lübbenau which lasts five hours and includes a boat ride.
Road B96. For further information apply to the regional tourist board: Fremdenverkehrsamt Lübbenau, Poststrasse 25; tel: 588 7223.

most people it is the most enjoyable way to see the truly remarkable scenery. The banks of the waterways heave under weeping willow, poplar and ash; marsh plants and tall grasses provide cover for white storks, waterfowl and even grass snakes, while the Spree's countless arteries yield prodigious quantities of eel, pike and perch, destined for the dining tables of local inns and guest houses. Further afield there is more to discover – enormous rounded haystacks resembling primitive huts, wooden-framed houses with the distinctive crossed-serpent pattern on their gables, village churches, ancient fortifications, craft shops and museums.

The history, customs and traditions of the local Sorb population, still very much alive, are fascinating and worth exploring.

Lübbenau

For information on boat trips (by paddle boat or punt), visit the tourist office (*Fremdenverkehrsamt*) at Poststrasse 25 or follow the signs advertising *Kahnfahrten* or *Paddleboten*. Lübbenau itself has a charming old town centre, which tends to get very crowded in season. Points of interest include the Marktplatz and the 18th-century church of St Nicholas; the Schloss, which dates from the Napoleonic period; and the Spreewald Museum near by, which provides a useful introduction to the region.

Spreewald Museum – open: May to October, Tuesday to Sunday 9am–5pm. Admission charge.

Lübben

The mainly baroque Paul-Gerhard-Kirche is worth seeing, as is the much older (and smaller) Steinkirchen (stone church)

dating from the beginning of the 13th century. Lübben also has its own Schloss and modest fortifications.

Bus from Lübbenau or train from Berlin Lichtenberg.

Lehde

The Freilichtsmuseum (open-air museum) describes the history and customs of the area and provides a fascinating insight into how the local farmhouses were constructed on the marshy ground.

30-minute walk from Lübbenau. Freilichts-museum – open: May to October, Tuesday to Sunday 9am–5pm. Admission charge.

Burg

Remote and therefore secluded, the local farmhouses here are the main attraction and there are good views from the Bismarckturm on top of the Schlossberg, just a couple of kilometres from the village.

Bus from Lübben.

Punting along the canals in Spreewald is a relaxing way to enjoy the area

WITTENBERG (Lutherstadt Wittenberg)

The name says it all. It was Martin Luther, then a university professor and monk, who put Wittenberg on the map in 1517 when he nailed his 95 theses to the door of the castle church, precipitating the Reformation, one of the most profound religious upheavals in history.

On the corner of Martin-Luther Strasse is the Luther Oak, commemorating the spot where, in December 1520, Father Martin publicly

defied the Pope by burning the Papal Bull threatening him with excommunication. In the 16th century Wittenberg was already famous for its university – both Shakespeare's Hamlet and Marlowe's Dr Faustus were students here. Scholars flocked to Wittenberg from all over Europe, outnumbering the permanent residents.

Lutherhaus

Luther's former monastery, the Lutherhaus on Collegienstrasse, is now a museum. Pass through the outer building into the imposing courtyard. Ahead is an immaculate white building with gabled roof, octagonal tower and an exquisite oriel window. The entrance is through a Renaissance doorway, the Katharinen portal, a birthday present from Luther to his wife in 1540. The highlight of the museum is Luther's private apartments which he shared with his wife, the former nun Katharina von Bora, and six children. Period furnishings, paintings, decorated wood panelling and unusual items like the tiled Renaissance stove in Luther's study convey the homeliness of Luther's family life. The other rooms on the first floor trace the dramatic life of the religious reformer and set it in the social and political context of the times. Aspects of the Catholic faith to which Luther later took exception – the proliferation of relics and the sale of indulgences – are illustrated by contemporary artefacts. There is also a copy of the Papal Bull of excommunication of 1520, a set of monks' robes and an absorbing and highly amusing assortment of anti-Papal propaganda. Famous artists like Dürer,

Martin Luther, the hero of Wittenberg, is commemorated in the Marktplatz

Holbein and Lucas Cranach the Elder were recruited for a highly professional campaign which concentrated on spreading the Lutheran message through the printed word. Support from intellectual big guns at the university like Phillip Melanchthon, and the protection of the Elector, Frederick the Wise, saved Luther from the stake, but only after he had spent several months on the run, adopting the alias Junke Jorg. On his triumphant return, Wittenberg became a centre of Lutheran religious experiment and the exhibition highlights some of the more striking aspects, the new priestly uniform and an experimental liturgy for example .

The ground floor is something of a miscellany. There is a concert hall with a fine vaulted ceiling – this was once the monks' refectory. Elsewhere is an exhibition on the history of the museum and on Wittenberg's historic links with printing, while the cellar contains a collection of medallions and coins, including a medal of Luther struck in 1521.
Open: Tuesday to Sunday 9am–5pm. Admission charge.

Market day in Wittenberg – little has changed over the centuries

Wittenberg town

In Luther's day the population of Wittenberg was only 2,000 and the entire length of the town stretched for less than a mile. The focal point is the stately and extremely photogenic Marktplatz with its magnificent, beautifully preserved town hall, a white gabled building with ornate portal dating from the 16th century. At that time it was the centre of town life with shops, a hall for dancing and concerts, and a tavern. The canopied statues framing it are – inevitably – of Luther and Melanchthon, the former by the Berlin architects Schadow and

Schinkel and dating from 1821. Dwarfing the houses on one side of the square are the twin towers of the Stadtkirche St Marien.

The 13th-century Town Church is Wittenberg's oldest building. Luther preached here and it was the first religious building to be adapted to the new Protestant rite. Its greatest artistic treasure is the large altar panel executed by the two Lucas Cranachs (older and younger) and completed in 1547.
Stadtkirche St Marien – open: daily 10am–noon, 2–5pm. Free.

Cranachhaus

The artist Lucas Cranach the Elder lived and worked here from 1513 to 1550 but not only as a painter – he was also an apothecary, a publisher, the owner of a printing press, a town councillor and even mayor! The extremely picturesque house and courtyard were only recently rescued from falling into ruin. There is a gallery and wine bar at the rear.

> Tourist Information: Collegienstrasse 28, Lutherstadt Wittenberg. Tel: (0451) 2239/2537.
> Trains every 2 hours from Bahnhof Berlin Lichtenberg.
> By road: E51/A9 to Coswig, then left on the B187.

Melanchthonhaus

Luther's second in command, famed throughout Europe as a humanist and Greek scholar, lived in this immaculately restored Renaissance house from 1536 to 1560. Stroll through the refurbished rooms, which include Melanchthon's study, and the period 'feel' is undeniable. The house is also a museum of university life, with student uniforms and fashion accessories from the 19th century. A more grisly exhibit is the hand of Susanne Zimmermann, who was broken on the wheel in 1728 for poisoning her stepchildren. Best to end on a happier note, with a look out over the garden where Frau Melanchthon was fond of growing herbs – part of the town wall is visible from here.

Martin Luther, instigator of one of the most profound religious upheavals in history

Open: Tuesday to Sunday 9am–5pm. Admission charge.

Schlosskirche

It was to the door of this, the castle church, that Martin Luther nailed his 95 theses on 31 October 1517. Sadly, both church and door were destroyed by soldiers during the Seven Years' War (1760). The present building is 19th-century and looks it, from the inside at least. Luther and Melanchthon are both buried here and replacement bronze doors, dating from 1858, commemorate the reformer's historic action. Climb the steps of the tower for splendid views over the River Elbe and surrounding countryside.

Open: daily 10am–noon, 2–5pm. Free.

GETTING AWAY FROM IT ALL

'Only quiet people live here,
eating their sandwiches
Under the lilac
while the boats go by.'
C H SISSON
Over the Wall: Berlin, May 1975

Getting Away From it All

CITY PARKS
Freizeit Park, Tegel

On the edge of the Tegeler Forest, more than 1,900 hectares of woodland, this is far and away Berlin's best out-of-town park. Attractions include an adventure playground, a paddling pool and trampolines; specially designated picnic and barbecue areas; table-tennis, volley-ball and chess. There are rowing boats and paddle boats for hire near the marina and cycles can also be hired out. All facilities are clearly signposted, with times of opening, and each of the main areas is zoned off by trees and pathways. A short walk away is the Greenwich promenade, where the English seaside theme extends eccentrically to red telephone kiosks and post boxes. Private yachts ply the waters here, competing with the pleasure cruisers. The firm of Reederei Heinz Riedel advertises daily tours of the Tegeler See and Heiligen See, departing about every two hours. Shops and cafés are close at hand in the attractively leafy suburb of Alt-Glienicke. *Boat to Greenwich Promenade or U-Bahn to Tegel.*

Tiergarten

This famous park, once a hunting ground for the Electors, is only a short distance away from the main sights around the Ku'damm (see pages 96–7 and 112). Technically you're only allowed to sunbathe on the designated areas but if in doubt follow the locals. A good stretch for lying out is in the vicinity of John-Foster-Dulles-Allee. Boats are available for hire near the Neuer See (the park's largest lake) and

A youngster mans the defences at Tegel's Greenwich promenade

there's a café here, too. Adorning the route from Tiergarten S-Bahn station into the park and down towards the Landwehrkanal is an unusual collection of gas-lamps from many of the major cities of Europe. Also near the canal, and with a fine view of the Siegessäule (Victory Column), is the attractive Löwenbrücke (Lion's bridge). Concerts take place in the summer (June to September) in the secluded Parkhaus of the Englischer Garten, which begins north of Altonaer Strasse. Berlin Zoo is virtually next door to the Tiergarten (entrance in Budapester Strasse).
U- or S-Bahn to Zoologischer Garten, or S-Bahn to Tiergarten.

Alt-Glienicke, near Tegel, is one of Berlin's most attractive suburbs

Treptower Park
The central feature of this sprawling park, dating from 1876, is the massive Sowjetisches Ehrenmal (Soviet War Memorial) commemorating the 5,000 soldiers killed during the capture of Berlin in 1945. The park is nowadays a favourite venue for funfairs.
S-Bahn to Treptower Park.

Viktoriapark
The park encompasses one of the highest points in Berlin (all of 66m!), the Kreuzberg (Mountain of the Cross). A series of steep terraces leads majestically to a masterpiece by Karl Friedrich Schinkel, his Monument to the Wars of Liberation (1813–15). Constructed from iron, this is a graceful neo-Gothic structure, culminating in a delicate spire. Militant angels guard the niches, while a sequence of plaques commemorates the various battles of the war. The monument was completed in 1821 and is all that survives of Schinkel's intention to build an enormous cathedral in honour of the Liberation on Leipzigerplatz. There is a children's playground in the park and the Golgotha café provides refreshment near the monument. Football teams from the Turkish league play here on Sundays.
U-Bahn to Platz der Luftbrücke.

Volkspark Friedrichshain
This attractive park, looking rather out of place in a heavily industrial and neglected area, was landscaped by P J Lenné in the mid-19th century. It is ideally suited to picnics and ball games but there is also an attractive rose garden and lake and a neo-baroque fountain, the Märchenbrunnen (Fable Fountain), designed by Ignaz Taschner and featuring characters from German fairy tales. Two artificial mounds, known as Trümmerberge, are composed of rubble from flak bunkers dating from World War II. Also in the park (on the south side) is the Friedhof der Märzgefallenen, a cemetery commemorating those who died fighting in the abortive revolutions of 1848 and 1918. The statue of Lenin which once stood near the park has been removed.
Am Friedrichshain. Trams 24, 28.

Grunewald – peace and quiet only half an hour's journey from the centre of Berlin

Grunewaldsee and around

Surrounded by woodland, peaceful except for the barking of dogs (Berlin claims to have more dogs than any other city in Europe) and teeming with wildlife, the Grunewaldsee is a gentle, 40-minute stroll from the main road. Just after Koenigs Allee you will see signs for the Hundekehlefenn nature reserve (the general term for a nature reserve is Naturschutzgebiet). Follow the footpath down to the lake and its sandy beaches, which are ideal for swimming. (There is a nudist beach on the western side, marked FKK on maps.) Picnicking is also allowed here.

Just south of the lake is the Fortshaus Paulsborn, a smart but demure restaurant with an attractive terrace.

Jagdschloss Grunewald

This is the hunting lodge built for the Elector Joachim II of Brandenburg in 1542. The outbuildings and stables were added later, beginning around 1700, and the original lodge was surrounded by a moat. The interior is decorated with paintings of hunting scenes, stuffed birds and stags' heads. Today the lodge is a museum, which includes a brief but pleasant tour. The Grosse Saal (Great Hall), with its magnificent wooden ceiling, is noteworthy because it is the only part of the original building to have survived. Most of the paintings were brought from other royal residences. Among the rather stiff portraits of the various Brandenburg rulers – and, somewhat incongruously, one of Julius Caesar by Rubens, acquired by the Great Elector – you will also find a Jordaens, a Brueghel and several

GRUNEWALD

Its literal meaning is the 'green forest' and there can be no more apt description for this immense (32sq km) tract of scenic woodland, interspersed with dappled paths, lakes, secluded beaches, nature reserves and country inns. In the 16th century the Grunewald took the fancy of the Elector Joachim II, who stocked it with wild boar, deer and other quarry and built a hunting lodge for himself and his guests. After World War II much of the forest, which consisted mainly of pine, was felled to provide fuel for the bombed-out population of Berlin; it was subsequently replaced with a more variegated mixture of beech, birch, oak and ash. Slicing through the middle of the forest is the Avus, a race track completed in 1921 and later turned into an autobahn.

paintings by Cranach the Elder, including a languid *Adam and Eve*. Cross the grassed-over cobbled courtyard to the barn, which has been converted into a hunting museum with all the paraphernalia of the chase. *Open: April to September 10am–6pm, March and October 10am–5pm, November to February 10am–4pm. Admission charge.*

Brücke-Museum
This modern art museum lies to the east of the Grunewaldsee, on Bussardsteig 9 (see pages 38–9).

Chalet Suisse
This Swiss-style cottage serves meals and snacks. There is a children's playground and a garden cluttered with fanciful model animals and even a make-believe old carriage. The finishing touch is a lady in folk costume playing an organ.

Grunewaldturm (Grunewald tower)
This folly on the banks of the Havel was designed by the architect of the Kaiser Wilhelm Memorial Church in 1897. The tower, which is 55m high, affords panoramic views across the Havel and the surrounding forest.

Krumme Lanke
A secluded lake suitable for swimming.

Langer Luchs (Long Lynx)
A marshy nature reserve, extending to the south of the Grunewaldsee.

Teufelsberg ('Devil's Mountain')
Despite appearances this 115m hill, lying north of the Grunewaldsee, is man-made. It was one of eight such mounds formed after World War II from the rubble cleared from Berlin's devastated buildings. Most of the work was done by women, who became known as *Trümmerfrauen*.

S-Bahn to Grunewald (Line 3). Bus 115 to Pückler Strasse.

Elector Joachim II's hunting lodge at Jagdschloss Grunewald

Friedrichshagen was founded in the 18th century by Frederick the Great

MÜGGELSEE

Traditionally the lakeside resorts and forests around the Grosser Müggelsee were a favourite weekend and summer haunt of East Berliners. With unification, however, this still beautiful area was deprived of its captive market and in future it will presumably have to compete with its Western rivals, Wannsee and Grunewald – no easy matter, as the facilities there are undeniably better. At the moment the Treuhand, the agency in charge of selling off former state-run enterpises, is looking for a buyer and the future of the resort is uncertain. What is certain, however, is that the Müggelsee itself will always attract visitors. The placid waters stretch over some 750 hectares, nearly three times the area of Wannsee, and the shores, with their reeds, water rushes, wild fowl, birds and wild flowers, are surprisingly unspoilt.

Rübezahl to the Teufelsee

The Gaststätten (restaurants), with their bleak concrete terraces have been closed for some time now, giving the place a somewhat forlorn look. It's possible to pick up the ferry here and cross the Müggelsee, but a more rewarding

WILHELM VOIGT

The local folk-hero is Wilhelm Voigt, a mischievous shoemaker and petty criminal who one day in 1906 dressed up as a captain in the Prussian army, commandeered a squad of grenadiers in Plötzensee, then marched them to Köpenick. Without once thinking to question his orders, the soldiers entered the town hall, arrested the mayor and handed over the contents of the treasury to Voigt, who promptly vanished. Voigt is commemorated in the local summer festival and you'll see images of the 'captain' outside buildings and bars all around Köpenick. Carl Zuckmayer's play *Der Hauptmann von Köpenick* (*The Captain of Köpenick*, retells the incident.

proposition might be to take the well-marked footpath to Teufelssee, the 'Devil's Lake', really little more than a pool surrounded by marsh and trees. Another footpath, marked Wanderlehrpfad, is a nature trail with indicators giving details of rocks, names of trees, birds etc. The path leading to the Müggelberge (a mound rather than a hill) ends at the Müggelturm, a look-out tower with wonderful views of the lakes and woods. Restaurants and bars abound but many are currently closed for renovation.
Bus 169 from Köpenick via Müggelheimer Damm.

Müggelseeperle

This sprawling holiday complex, a stone's throw along the lake from Rübezahl, is currently in the same state of limbo. Ferries arrive at the pier here from Friedrichshagen before returning to Berlin via Treptow and Steglitz.

Friedrichshagen

This small, attractive town was founded in the 18th century by Frederick the Great as a settlement for cotton spinners. More than 100 Bohemian families were invited to colonise the area on condition that they took responsibility for planting mulberry trees for rearing silk worms. Friedrichshagen retains a village atmosphere, especially in the neighbourhood of Bölschestrasse, where some of the mulberry trees and original houses are still to be seen. Look out, too, for the 19th-century restaurant, Zum Maulbeerbaum, which has a reputation for traditional German cooking. Writers like Frank Wedekind, author of *Lulu* (later set to music by Alban Berg) and Gerhard Hauptmann found the atmosphere here congenial.

Not far away, along the Müggelseedamm, is the Wasserwerk Friedrichshagen, a neo-Gothic brick waterworks now converted to a museum illustrating the history of the Müggelsee in supplying Berlin with water. On the western fringes of the lake, at Fürstenwalder Damm, is an FKK (nudist beach).
S-Bahn line 3, two stops after Köpenick.

Rahnsdorf

The attraction here is the old fishing village, where fishermen's houses cluster around the lakeside and the parish church.
S-Bahn line 3, one stop after Friedrichshagen, then bus 161 for 6 stops.

Enjoy traditional German cuisine at 19th-century Zum Maulbeerbaum in Friedrichshagen

WANNSEE

This stunning lakeside resort on the western fringes of Berlin offers every imaginable diversion – beaches, tennis, golf, water sports, river cruises, scenic walks and numerous places of interest.

Boat trips and excursions

The possibilities are endless. From Wannsee Bridge pier there are tours of Wannsee Island and excursions to Potsdam, Spandau, the Tegeler See and points around the Havel. Visitors with a BVG pass can take the ferry to Kladow – the most economical way to enjoy the magnificent views.

Blockhaus Nikolskoe

See page 31.
Bus 216 from Wannsee station.

Kleist's grave

A plain granite stone strewn with flowers marks the site where the Romantic poet, Heinrich von Kleist, committed suicide with his lover and companion, Henriette Vogel, on 21 November 1811 (see page 57). The inscription reads: 'Now, oh immortality, are you wholly mine'. The grave is situated in woodland over-looking the shores of Kleiner Wannsee, off Bismarck Strasse and very near the station.

Pfaueninsel

Peacock Island is an enjoyable, five-minute ferry ride from the opposite bank (small charge). It was acquired by Frederick William II in 1793 as a hideaway for himself and his mistress. Sad to say, premature death through the unlikely accident of being hit in the eye with a champagne cork cut short his enjoyment. It was his successor Frederick William III who turned the island into the idiosyncratic nature reserve it is today. The terrain is populated not only by wildlife but by numerous follies, the most prominent of which is a white-brick ruined castle, the Schloss, constructed in 1794. The island is a special protection area so there are no refreshments on sale and picnicking is confined to one designated area. But wander at leisure and enjoy a mock-Gothic farm with real geese, an entertaining bird reserve and, down by the pier, a miniature frigate presented by King George IV of England – and the peacocks, of course!

Schloss Glienicke

See page 57.
Bus 116 from Wannsee station.

Strandbad Wannsee

Once glamorous and still popular with Berliners, this is the largest inland beach in Europe. Facilities include changing rooms, sun terraces, shops, eateries, slides, diving boards, a jetty, even life-sized chess. The entrance is well signposted from Nikolskoe station. Admission charge.

Wannsee Conference House

The mottled grey villa with beautiful views across the lake was once owned by a wealthy industrialist, Friedrich Minoux. It was still known as the Villa Minoux in 1940 when it was acquired by the SS as a guest house. On 20 January 1942 the head of the Reich Central Security Office, Reinhard Heydrich, summoned leading SS officers and civil servants here to discuss the implementation of the policy of deportation and mass murder of up to 11 million European Jews.

Ring the bell at the main gate for

entry – owing to the attentions of neo-Nazis, the curators have had to adopt tight security measures.

The permanent exhibition is set out in 14 rooms and traces the whole horrifying story, from the origins of the Nazi dictatorship through the deportations, setting up of extermination camps and annihilation of the Jews to their belated deliverance at the end of the war. Whole rooms are devoted to Auschwitz and the Warsaw Ghetto Uprising. But the focal point of the display is Room 6, where the conference itself took place. The conference minutes, which reveal an almost pedantic obsession with organisational niceties, are in the hand of Adolf Eichmann, who was eventually brought to justice by an Israeli court in 1962 and subsequently executed.

An English language leaflet is available at the information desk. Admission free.

Am Grossen Wannsee 58. Open: Monday to Friday 10am–6pm, Sunday 2–6pm. Free. Bus 114 from Wannsee station.

The white-brick Schloss is one of many follies on Peacock Island

MÜRITZ NATIONAL PARK

To get away from it all, head north of Berlin for Germany's largest nature reserve. Its centrepiece, the Müritz National Park, was created in 1990 and extends over an area of more than 300sq km, from Waren in the north to Neustrelitz in the east and Wittstock, the source of the Havel, in the south. A place of extraordinary natural beauty, Müritz is easily accessible by car (take route E 96 from Berlin) but on arrival it is much more rewarding to explore its riches on foot, taking any of the numerous and well-signposted pathways. The Müritzsee is only one of 117 lakes in the park, though, stretching as it does for more than 27km, it is the second largest lake in Germany. In the winter this is an inhospitable landscape, bleak and windswept, the marshes, more

The meadows support many varieties of rare flowers, including the heath spotted orchid

often than not, shrouded in mist, hospitable terrain only for white-tailed eagles and black storks. In the summer the lakes appear placid and benign – insects thrive among the breeding grounds of cranes and grey herons. Small oases of moorland and meadow support numerous varieties of rare grasses and wild flowers, orchids and gentians among them, and numerous species of butterfly have been identified. White unhorned cattle and sheep graze here, too. Nearly two-thirds of the land consists of mixed forest, predominantly firs, alders and birches, the perfect habitat for wild deer.

While the pleasures of the National Park are inexhaustible, there is nothing to stop the visitor straying further afield, to the attractive towns of Neustrelitz and Wesenberg, for example – towns of Slav origin in a region which was first settled in Mesolithic times. When the naturalists depart, in come the archaeologists to discover the region's fascinating past. Recent finds include jewellery from the Bronze Age and Roman silverware.

The marshes of Müritz National Park are an ideal habitat for the great heron

DIRECTORY

'Anyone who can build toilets like this
is capable of anything.'

ERICA JONG,
Fear of Flying

Shopping

*A*s a shopping Mecca Berlin is unrivalled. The Kurfürstendamm (Ku'damm), nearly 4km long, is the main shopping street and no visitor need stray very far from here to find everything they need. Tired and hungry shoppers will be relieved to find that there are dozens of cafés, *imbiss* stands and restaurants in the neighbourhood.

The streets off the Ku'damm, especially Bleibtreustrasse and Pariser Strasse, are famous for fashion boutiques (not all the shops are exclusive, however), while Kantstrasse has a reputation for clothing bargains. Antique shops (Berlin currently specialises in art deco) can be found in Goethestrasse, Pestalozzistrasse and Fasanenstrasse. The city's main department stores are also close at hand. Wertheim's is on the Ku'damm itself, across the road from the Europa-Center; KaDeWe (Kaufhaus des Westens) and Peek and Cloppenburg are around the corner in Wittenbergplatz. For an alternative to the Ku'damm, take the U-Bahn to Adenauerplatz and try the Wilmersdorferstrasse, a more compact and pedestrianised shopping area which offers a good range of shops, including several stores – Hertie, for example.

Shopping on the east side
Since Unification, Western-style shops have been opening all over former East Berlin, mainly boutiques and hi-tech stores. But the prices are way beyond the reach of locals – many of the smart shops in Schönhauser Allee and Prenzlauer

Berlin is an antique collector's dream with so many places to choose from

Berg, for example, are virtually empty. Presumably the situation will change over the next 10 years, when several massive shopping and office developments are due to open on the eastern side – around Alexanderplatz for example, and in the Friedrichstadt Passage (scheduled to open in 1995). Prices in the newer stores are no more competitive than those in the West; however, private enterprise is also showing its face in the rapidly increasing numbers of market stalls which you'll find outside S-Bahn stations and along individual shopping streets in the remoter neighbourhoods. Clothing and other items here can be relatively cheap. It's certainly worth keeping an eye open for bargains.

Best buys

Souvenirs can be found in plentiful supply along the Ku'damm. T-shirts with Berlin emblems and logos are always a hit with teenagers and are not overly expensive. Shops at the museums sell notebooks, pens and other cheap items ideal for children to take back to friends. For the political tourist, chunks of concrete purporting to be pieces of the Berlin wall are still on sale around Checkpoint Charlie and the Brandenburg Gate, at varying prices, depending on size. Don't kid yourself that you're buying the real thing, although you may just strike lucky – certainly don't pay more for a 'certificated' piece – the certificates are bogus. Eastern bloc *memorabilia* is also readily available: everything from caps, belts and badges to greatcoats sporting the proper insignia, and East German flags. All this paraphernalia is more likely to be authentic having been sold off by departing or de-mobbed troops –

No German city is more fashion-conscious than Berlin

but, again, you can never be sure. For a more up-market memento of your visit, shop for porcelain made in the KPM factory in Berlin or the more expensive Meissen variety, or look out for table linen, silverware or bed-covers. Cameras are also a good buy, as are toys, for which the Germans are famous.

Bargains

The best place for bargains is the weekend market on Strasse des 17 Juni (S-Bahn Tiergarten) where you'll find a wide range of items, from books to fancy jewellery. Nollendorf flea market is another good source of cheap and second-hand goods. Finally, for second-hand clothing it's worth a trek out to Garage in Nollendorf (Ahornstrasse 2), which is said to be Europe's biggest store of its kind.

Market browsing is the perfect antedote to sight-seeing blues

SHOPPING HOURS

Most shops are open Monday to Friday from 9.30am to 6.30pm, but Saturday shopping is only from 9am to 2pm, except on the first Saturday of the month and weekends leading up to Christmas, when shops stay open until 6pm. Late-night shopping is Thursday, when a number of stores stay open until 8pm. Early Saturday closing means that the shops become very crowded in the course of the morning, so it's best to avoid them altogether.

VAT

Anyone buying more than 60DM worth of goods from any one shop and intending to take them out of the country is entitled to a rebate on the VAT (in German, *Mehrwertsteuer*). Simply fill out a form in the store, then, on leaving Germany, present it, along with the item and the receipt, to customs. Note that the rebate will be 6 to 11 per cent of the purchase price and not the full value of VAT.

ANTIQUES
Astoria
Art deco jewellery, statues, mirrors, lamps, tables; expensive but some cheaper replicas available.
Bleibtreustrasse 50. Tel: 3128304.
Zille Hoff
Pots and pans, furniture, glasses, books, old clothes, bric-à-brac.
Fasanenstrasse 14. Tel: 3134333.

BOOKS
Kiepert
All subjects. Good on travel.
Hardenbergstrasse 4–5. Tel: 3110090.
Marga Schoeller
The best shop for books in English and for German language books on Berlin.
Knesebeckstrasse 33–4. Tel: 8811112.

CLOTHES
Hennes and Mauritz
Swedish clothes chain with cheap up-to-date clothes.
Kurfürstendamm 20. Tel: 8826299.
Molotow
Clothes by Berlin designers at average to expensive prices.
Gneisenaustrasse 112. Tel: 693813.

DEPARTMENT STORES
KaDeWe
Tauentzienstrasse 21. Tel: 21210.
Wertheim
Kurfürstendamm 231. Tel: 882061.
Hertie
Wilmersdorferstrasse 118. Tel: 311050.

JEWELLERY
Maria Makkaroni
Fun jewellery, costumes and accessories.
Bleibtreustrasse 49. Tel: 3128584.
Rio
Smart and sophisticated, with prices to match.
Bleibtreustrasse 52. Tel: 3133152.

MARKETS
Strasse des 17 Juni
Ideal for picking up gifts, especially embroidery, lace, ethnic jewellery and art work – everything, in fact.
Tel: 3228199. Open: weekends.
Nollendorfplatz U-Bahn
Flea market.
Open: 11am–7pm. Closed: Tuesday.
Winterfeldmarkt
Where Berliners shop. Ideal for whiling away a Saturday morning, with plenty of cafés to hand.
Winterfeldplatz. Open: Wednesday and Saturday 8am–1pm.

PERFUME
Harry Lehmann
A family business where you can even bring your own bottle.
Kantstrasse 106. Tel: 3243582.

Thinking of the folks back home? Souvenir mugs make an ideal gift

The Sunday market, Strasse des 17 Juni

PORCELAIN
KPM
Pottery manufactured by the famous Royal Porcelain Factory, founded in the 18th century by Frederick the Great.
Kurfürstendamm 26a. Tel: 8811802.

SPORT
Ozone
Everything for the sporting man and woman.
Knesebeckstrasse 27.

TOYS
Heidi's Spielzeugladen
Specialises in traditional German toys, including puppets and wooden train sets.
Kantstrasse 61. Tel: 3237556.
Berliner Zinnfiguren
An amazing array of hand-made tin soldiers.
Knesebeckstrasse 88. Tel: 310802.

FILM

Berlin's love affair with the silver screen began in 1895, when the brothers Max and Emil Skladanowsky showed a primitive film at the Wintergarten using the world's first projector, the bioscope. The first cinema arrived just four years later in an otherwise anonymous building on Münzstrasse.

During World War I the propaganda needs of the army gave birth to a German film industry whose financing was masterminded by the Chief of Staff, General Erich Ludendorff. UFA (Universum Film Aktiengesellschaft) began making patriotic features in purpose-built studios in Babelsberg near Potsdam. Films were also made in Schöneberg. The heyday of UFA came in the 1920s with a succession of classic films, including *Dr Caligari*, the futuristic fantasy *Metropolis* – a spectacular flop at the box office – and *The Blue Angel*, which became the vehicle for a rising young starlet, Marlene Dietrich.

Under the Nazis, UFA became the tool and plaything of Hitler's propaganda chief, Josef Goebbels. Goebbels used the casting couch to get his way with beautiful young hopefuls, while hiring big names like

Werner Krauss to star in unashamedly anti-semitic films, most notoriously *Jud Süss*. Meanwhile, the actress-turned-filmmaker Leni Riefenstall, was making her two classic propaganda pageants for Hitler, *Der Triumph des Willens* (Triumph of the Will), a cine-montage of the 1934 Nuremberg party rally, and *Olympia*, eulogising the Berlin Olympic Games of 1936. Hitler himself was never portrayed on screen except in the guise of the model Prussian, Frederick the Great. But to win the

hearts and minds of German cinema audiences it was necessary to resort to pure, unadulterated entertainment. During the dark days of the war, escapist Hollywood-style fantasies soothed the nerves of a gloomy and apprehensive population.

In recent years, Berlin itself has been the

Rainer Werner Fassbinder's
epic masterpiece at the
Goethe-Institut London

Berlin Alexanderplatz

'It poses the
central question:
is there a life
before death?'
Peter Buchka, 12.10.90

**All-weekend screening
9/10/11 October 1992**
'... the ultimate achievement
of the New German Cinema.'
Andreas Kilb, 12.6.92

star of a number of films, including Wim Wender's *Wings of Desire* and Rainer Werner Fassbinder's epic *Berlin Alexanderplatz*, the longest commercially released film on record at 15 hours 21 minutes. Many of Germany's most original post-war film directors, including Wenders and Fassbinder, trained at the UFA studios before going on to make their careers elsewhere.

Film remains something of an obsession with Berliners and the city's international film festival, held in February, is second in importance only to the Venice Biennale.

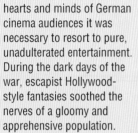

Berlin was once the capital of Germany's film industry

Entitertainment and Nightlife

*B*erlin thrives on an embarrassment of cultural riches and the range could not be more eclectic – from Grand Opera to *Phantom of the Opera*, from symphony concerts to rock concerts. There's contemporary and classical dance, theatre of every conceivable variety, a feast of film, and discos and night clubs for those with the necessary stamina. The fun extends from dusk to dawn, for Berlin is a city that never sleeps.

Theatre is a highly competitive business in Berlin with so much to choose from

director, Max Reinhardt and superb actresses like Lotte Lenya and Elisabeth Bergner. Currently the theatres are in crisis, as the Senate tries to reduce the huge budget deficit – the prestigious Schiller Theatre is faced with losing its subsidy entirely, although there has been a fierce rearguard action to save it. There are few, if any productions in English.

TICKET AGENCIES
Berlin Ticket im KaDeWe
Tauentzienstrasse. Tel: 241028.
City Center
Kurfürstendamm 16. Tel: 8826563.
Kant-Kasse
Kantstrasse 54. Tel: 3134554.

LISTINGS MAGAZINES
Tip and *Zitty* appear twice monthly – comprehensive but unwieldy, and in German.
Berlin Programm – a monthly, also in German but more manageable.
Checkpoint – an English-language monthly, useful but highly selective.

THEATRE
The golden age of the Berlin theatres was the 1920s and '30s, when the dominating figures included the playwrights Bertolt Brecht and Carl Zuckmayer, the great

Berliner Ensemble
Brecht's famous theatre, still specialising in his plays and others in the radical tradition.
Am Bertolt-Brecht-Platz. Tel: 2823160.
U- or S-Bahn to Friedrichstrasse.
Deutsches Theater
Max Reinhardt directed here; classical repertoire.
Schumannstrasse 13. Tel: 28441225.
U- or S-Bahn to Friedrichstrasse.
Metropol-Theater
Musicals like *Evita* and *West Side Story* are performed here.
Friedrichstrasse (near the station).
Tel: 20364117. U- or S-Bahn to Friedrichstrasse.
Schaubühne am Lehniner Platz
Reputation for innovative and experimental modern drama.
Kurfürstendamm 153. Tel: 890023.

U-Bahn to Adenauerplatz.
Theater des Westerns
Broadway shows, musicals.
Kantstrasse 12. Tel: 8822888. U- or S-Bahn to Zoologischer Garten.

CABARET AND VARIETY

Any one hoping to catch a glimpse of cabaret as it was in the Berlin of the 1920s is liable to be disappointed, though attempts to revive the earlier variety-music hall tradition with circus acts etc have fared somewhat better. Transvestite shows are popular here and even if they're not generally to your taste you may like to sample one, if only to see what all the fuss is about. Political satire is still very much part of the Berlin cabaret scene, but, needless to say, you'll need excellent German to appreciate all the nuances – or even to get the point at all. If you think you fit the bill, consult the listings magazines – the choice is limitless.

BKA–Berliner Kabarett Anstalt
Alternative cabaret in Kreuzberg, popular with Berliners.
Mehringdamm 32–4. Tel: 2510112. U-Bahn to Mehringdamm.
Chez Nous
Transvestite show.
Marburger Strasse 14. Tel: 2131810.

U-Bahn to Kurfürstendamm or Wittenbergplatz.
Die Distel
Formerly scourge of the GDR establishment, now casting a satirical eye over unified Germany.
Friedrichstrasse 107. Tel: 2004704. U- or S-Bahn to Friedrichstrasse.
Friedrichstadtpalast
Glitzy floor show with music, dance, circus acts etc.
Friedrichstrasse 107. Tel: 28466474. U- or S-Bahn to Friedrichstrasse.
La Vie en Rose
Glamorous show-girls in feathers and pearls.
Europa-Center. Tel: 3236006. U- or S-Bahn to Zoologischer Garten.
Wintergarten
Following on an old variety tradition.
Potsdamer Strasse 96. Tel: 2627070/ 2616060. U-Bahn to Kurfürstenstrasse.

ALTERNATIVE
UFA-fabrik
The place to go for alternative events of all kinds – musical, theatrical, film, dance.
Viktoriastrasse 13, Kreuzberg. Tel: 7528085. U-Bahn to Ullsteinstrasse.

Cabaret new-style – showgirls and glamour at La Vien en Rose

The Classical-style Deutsche Staatsoper, at Unter den Linden

MUSIC

Berlin has an enviable musical tradition going back to 1791 and the founding of the Singakademie. The young composer Felix Mendelssohn led the rediscovery of the music of J S Bach with a performance of the *St Matthew Passion* in the 1840s. Later in the century Liszt, Berlioz and Wagner all appeared in Berlin but the city is most famous for the Berlin Philharmonic Orchestra, founded in 1882 and still gracing the city today.

JAZZ/FOLK

Blues Café
Classical jazz.
Körnerstrasse 11. Tel: 2613698. U-Bahn to Kurfürstenstrasse.

Go In
Increasingly popular international folk venue.
Bleibtreustrasse 17. Tel: 8817218. S-Bahn to Savignyplatz.

Irish Inn
Folk and Guinness served up in good measure by boisterous Celts.
Damaschkestrasse 28. S-Bahn to Charlottenburg.

Quasimodo
For jazz lovers with eclectic tastes.
Kantstrasse 12a. Tel: 3128086. U-Bahn to Zoologischer Garten.

OPERA/BALLET

Deutsche Oper Berlin
A great opera tradition, despite artless modern venue – also modern ballet.
Bismarckstrasse 35, Charlottenburg. Tel: 3410249. U-Bahn to Deutsche Oper.

Deutsche Staatsoper
Classical opera and ballet in a classical

setting, the opera directed by eminent conductor and pianist Daniel Barenboim.
Unter den Linden 7. Tel: 2004762. U- and S-Bahn to Friedrichstrasse. Bus 101.

Komische Oper
Operettas and ballet
Behrenstrasse 55–7. Tel: 2292555. U-Bahn to Französische Strasse. Bus 100.

ROCK/POP

Deutschlandhalle
Popular venue for rock concerts.
Messedamm 26. Tel: 30381. S-Bahn to Westkreuz.

Eissporthalle Jaffestrasse
Rock bands with an international reputation often play here.
Charlottenburg. Tel: 30384444. S-Bahn to Westkreuz.

ICC Berlin (International Congress Centre)
Often used for pop concerts.
Messedamm 26. Tel: 30380. U-Bahn to Kaiserdamm. S-Bahn to Westkreuz. Buses 104, 105, 110, 149, 219.

Waldbühme
Germany's largest open-air arena, near the Olympic Stadium: spectacular venue for summer concerts – rock bands perform here, but also opera stars like Placido Domingo.
Glockenturmstrasse/Passenheimer Strasse 1/19. Tel: 3040676.

SYMPHONY/CHAMBER CONCERTS

Kammermusiksaal
Part of the Philharmonie complex, this smaller hall is used for chamber concerts.
Matthäikirchstrasse 1. Tel: 254880. S-Bahn to Potsdamer Platz. Buses 129, 148, 248, 348.

Philharmonie
Scharoun's masterpiece, this wonderful modern auditorium is the home of the world-famous Berlin Philharmonic.
Matthäikirchstrasse 1. Tel: 254880. S-Bahn to Potsdamer Platz. Buses 129, 148, 248, 348.

Schauspielhaus Berlin
Home of the Berlin Symphony Orchestra, though other orchestras play here too.
Gendarmenmarkt 2. Tel: 20902129/56. U-Bahn Französische Strasse or Hausvogteiplatz.

OTHER VENUES

Tempodrom
Two giant tents in the Tiergarten in summer, hosting all kinds of live music, including pop and jazz.
Tel: 3944045.

Rock musician at the Ku'damm

CABARETS AND REVUES

'Life is a cabaret' declares Sally Bowles in Bob Fosse's 1972 film. And for some, life in 1920s Berlin was, indeed, one long round of parties, champagne, jazz music and every conceivable kind of hedonistic pleasure. Certainly Berlin lived up to its reputation as a Mecca of vice, Sodom and Gomorrah rolled into one. Decadent and dangerous, Berlin

invited its children to 'Take a walk on the wild side'. Every imaginable sexual taste was catered for. For homosexuals there were the Kleistkasino and the clubs around Nollendorfplatz – still the centre of the gay scene today. Lesbians, attired in dinner jackets and

monocles, headed for the Mali club, while the transvestites' favourite haunt was the Eldorado. Those with more conventional tastes were not disappointed either. At the Apollo Theatre on Friedrichstrasse, scantily clad girls posed in sacrilegious imitation of the goddess of peace and her acolytes on top of the Brandenburg Gate. For the less artistically minded there were the dance troops – the Tiller girls at the Scala, for example. Or one could go to the Resi (Residenzcasino) on Alexanderplatz, where each table was provided with a telephone for flirting with fellow diners.

But conspicuous wealth and loose living was not the whole story. Liza Minelli's portrayal of Sally Bowles may be an artistic *tour de force*, but it was not true to life. The real Sally was a struggling English cabaret singer called Jean Ross, who appeared in the seediest nightclubs while sharing the 'life of the unemployed' with the writer, Christopher Isherwood and his friends W H Auden and Stephen Spender. At least Marlene Dietrich's

Marlene Dietrich was a cabaret chorus girl before starring in the *Blue Angel*

performance in *The Blue Angel* was drawn from experience. She was in the back row of the chorus line of a revue on the Ku'damm when she was talent-spotted by an associate of the director Joseph von Sternberg. The film made her career and she was soon off to Hollywood.

Since 1989 a concerted effort has been made to revive the old cabaret tradition, albeit shorn of sexual and other excesses. Perhaps it is all rather tame by comparison with the 1920s but there is plenty of variety: women impersonators, glitzy showgirls, circus acts and political satire. The motivation is the same for all. It's money, after all, that 'makes the world go round'.

CINEMA

Berlin became the capital of Germany's cinema industry in the early 1920s with the founding of the UFA studios in Babelsberg. The Berlin Film Festival, held in February, is the time to see the best in international films. All films are dubbed unless indicated by OF (films in the original without subtitles) or OmU (original soundtrack with German subtitles). The following cinemas show films in English:

Arsenal
Welserstrasse 25. Tel: 2186848. U-Bahn to Viktoria-Luise-Platz.
Babylon
Dresdner Strasse 126. Tel: 6146316. U-Bahn to Kotbusser Tor.
Delphi
Kantstrasse 12a. Tel: 3121026. U- or S-Bahn to Zoologischer Garten.
Film Palast
Kurfürstendamm 225. Tel: 8838551. U-Bahn to Adenauer Platz.

Odeon
Hauptstrasse 116. Tel: 7815667. U-Bahn to Kleistpark or Innsbrucker Platz.

NIGHT CLUBS/DISCOS

The scene, like everywhere else, is constantly changing. Refreshingly, most clubs charge only a small entry fee or none at all, though drink prices are predictably steep. Discos and clubs stay open late or very late. The following is necessarily a tiny selection: if you prefer to go on spec and take pot luck, wander around the Ku'damm at midnight and see where you best fit in. Kreuzberg has an excellent late-night scene – for night clubs try Oranienstrasse.

Big Eden
Living on past glories, very loud, very crowded but lively. For the very young! *Kurfürstendamm 202. Tel: 8826120. U-Bahn to Uhlandstrasse.*

Babylon Cinema, Dresdner Strasse

Rock around the clock in the Eden disco in Kurfürstendamm

Café Keese
Fun for ageing ravers. Strict dress code – collar and tie advisable for gents. Live band.
Bismarckstrasse 108. Tel: 3129111.
U-Bahn to Ernst-Reuter-Platz.

Cha Cha
Trendy, popular with those in the know.
Nürnberger Strasse 50. Tel: 2142976.
U-Bahn to Wittenbergplatz.

Dschungel
Established reputation, popular with locals.
Nürnberger Strasse 53. Tel: 2186698.
U-Bahn to Wittenbergplatz.

Metropol
Very popular weekend venue with Berliners in a famous art deco theatre.
Nollendorfplatz 5. Tel: 2164122. U-Bahn Nollendorfplatz.

Sox
Popular Kreuzberg hot-spot.
Oranienstrasse 39. Tel: 6143573. U-Bahn Schlesisches Tor.

CASINO
Spielbank Berlin
Europa-Center. Tel: 2500890. U-Bahn to Kurfürstendamm, U- or S-Bahn to Zoologischer Garten.

Summer nights in Berlin, all the fun of the fair

Villa Grisebach, a Jugendstil palace now housing the Galerie Pels-Leusden

GALLERIES AND EXHIBITIONS

One of the first business ventures to revive after the end of World War II was the commercial art market. Today there are around 150 galleries in Berlin dealing in paintings, sculptures, ceramics, posters, graphics and photographs. The auction houses Christies and Sothebys also have branches in the city. There are two distinct areas, geographically and commercially. The galleries in the streets off the Ku'damm, particularly Fasanenstrasse, Knesebeckstrasse and Wielandstrasse, specialise in the work of established contemporary artists and in the art of the late 19th and early 20th centuries. The old working class suburbs of Kreuzberg, Scheunenviertel and Prenzlauer Berg are home to galleries featuring up-and-coming artists, as well as those who have chosen to reject the commercial market entirely in favour of co-operative ventures.

Visiting the galleries around the Ku'damm does not entail spending vast sums of money – the entertainment lies in seeing just what is on offer. It is worth bearing in mind, for example, that one is more likely to come across artists from the German Expressionist movement and the Neue Sachlichkeit (New Objectivity), names like Dix, Kirchner, Heckel and Liebermann, in the auction rooms of Fasanenstrasse than in the city's public galleries. The sale rooms of the Villa Grisebach regularly turn up work by the famous German Romantic artist, Menzel, as well as Klee and Nolde, while the equally famous Brusberg Gallery might be exhibiting artists of the stature of Dali, Max Ernst and even Picasso. The ambience of these galleries is in itself relaxing and enjoyable – there is a cultivated atmosphere in the 19th-century drawing rooms of the Jugendstil villas of Fasanenstrasse, architectural monuments in their own right. And some galleries, like the Bremer, even have an evening bar scene where it is possible to see the market at work.

Kreuzberg and the other districts mentioned earlier offer a completely different experience. Here, little-known but talented artists exhibit their work in *ateliers* carved out of old bakeries, warehouses and factories and the exhibitions, invariably informal, are often accompanied by various kinds of 'happening' involving anything from music to mime. Prenzlauer Berg, formerly in East Germany, was a centre of political radicalism and alternative culture, and the artists here are now anxiously coming to terms with the implications of unification. The best way of exploring the alternative scene is simply to wander the streets. Try Curvy Strasse in Kreuzberg, the Hakeschen Höfen near Oranienburger Strasse in the Scheunenviertel and Tucholskystrasse and Augstrasse in Prenzlauer Berg.

Berlin Programm has a special section devoted to galleries, giving up-to-date information on current exhibitions.

Around the Ku'damm
Galerie Bremer
Specialises in established modern German artists.
Fasanenstrasse 37. Tel: 8814908. Open: Tuesday to Friday noon–6pm, Saturday 11am–1pm. U-Bahn to Uhlandstrasse.

Galerie Brusberg
Contemporary painting and sculpture occasionally featuring 20th-century masters like Picasso and Miró.
Kurfürstendamm 213. Tel: 8827682. Open: Tuesday to Friday 10am–6.30pm, Saturday 10am–2pm. U-Bahn to Uhlandstrasse.

Galerie Fahnemann
For anyone interested in Pop Art.
Fasanenstrasse 61. Tel: 8812157. Open: Tuesday to Friday 1–6.30pm, Saturday 11am–2pm. U-Bahn to Spichernstrasse.

Galerie Pels-Leusden (Villa Grisebach)
Next to the Käthe Kollwitz museum, specialises in art from the 19th and 20th centuries, especially German.
Villa Grisebach, Fasanenstrasse 25. Tel:

8859150. Open: Monday to Friday 10am–6.30pm, Saturday 10am–2pm. U-Bahn to Uhlandstrasse.

Other areas
Galerie im Scheunenviertel
Weinmeisterstrasse 8. Tel: 2817332. Open: Monday to Friday 2–6pm, Saturday noon–5pm. U-Bahn to Weinmeisterstrasse.

Galerie Wohnmaschine
Tucholskystrasse 34. Tel: 2815812. Open: Tuesday, Wednesday, Friday, Saturday 2–7pm, Thursday 5–9pm. S-Bahn to Oranienburger Strasse.

Hakeschen Höfen
The artists' studios are dotted about the restored warehouses and visitors are welcome.
Rosenthaler Strasse, Mitte. S-Bahn to Hakescher Markt.

Mora Café-Galerie
Grossbeerenstrasse 57a, Kreuzberg. Tel: 7850585. Open: daily 11am–1am. U-Bahn to Mehringdamm.

Still life with nude, glazed tile and fruit at Villa Grisebach

Children

BOAT TRIPS

There are boat stops at regular intervals along the Spree so one can act on impulse. See pages 114–15.

GENERAL SPORTS FACILITIES

The Sport und Erhohlungszentrum (SEZ) in Landsberger Allee is unbeatable but probably best suited to older children. There is a roller-skating centre in the Hasenheide (U-Bahn Hermannplatz), where skate hire is available.

MUSEUMS

The Museum für Naturkunde has a gigantic dinosaur skeleton to marvel at as well as other attractions. The Museum für Völkerkunde (Ethnography Museum – see page 48) has a rich and stimulating ethnological collection, including masks, canoes, reconstructed dwellings and weapons. If you're visiting the Dahlem Museums there's a section specially designed for children. Older children will appreciate the Haus am Checkpoint Charlie (see page 58), an entertaining account of the history of the Wall with the emphasis on escapology. Another favourite is the Museum für Verkehr und Technik (Trasnport and Technology Museum, see page 78) with its collections of vintage cars, aeroplanes and steam trains. The Panoptikum (Waxworks Museum) has the added advantage of being on the Ku'damm, as does the intriguing Teddy Museum Berlin (see pages 70–1).
Museum für Naturkunde, Invalidenstrasse 43. Tel: 28972540. Open: Tuesday to Sunday 9am–5pm. U- or S-Bahn to Friedrichstrasse.

OUT OF TOWN

There are acres of woodland around Berlin where children can romp and let off steam. Wannsee (S-Bahn to Nikolassee) and Müggelsee (S-Bahn to Friedrichshagen or Rahnsdorf) both have beaches; or there are the lakeside beaches in Grunewald – ideal for picnics and with nature trails to hand. Also in Grunewald is the Chalet Suisse, with its novelty garden. While in Wannsee, visit Peacock Island, where the animals and follies will keep children amused.

PARKS

Freizeitpark Tegel offers enough for children to do for at least half a day and there is the additional possibility of boat rides (see page 132).

Children making the most of the Neptune Fountain, near Marienkirche

Keeping children entertained in Berlin is made easy

PLAYGROUNDS

There is no shortage of playgrounds in Berlin. The following is just a selection:

Near Savignyplatz station
Ludwigkirchplatz (off the Ku'damm) with toddler playground, garden and fountain.

Tiergarten, near the Stuhlerstrasse entrance
Käthe Kollwitz Platz.

Monbijou Park, near Museum Island

SWIMMING POOLS

For children under the age of 14 the Kinderschwimmbad am Monbijouplatz (entrance on Oranienburger Strasse) is ideal because of its situation, right next door to Museum Island.

BLUB describes itself as a swimming paradise with fountains, waterfalls, wave pool and a 120m-long 'superslide'.
Buschkrugallee 64. Tel: 6066060. Open: daily 10am–11pm, Saturday and Sunday 9am–midnight. U-Bahn to Grenzallee.

ZOOS

Naturally Berlin has two! The Berlin Zoo (U- or S-Bahn Zoologischer Garten, entrance in Budapester Strasse) was founded in the 1840s but much of the stock was wiped out by wartime bombing. The Aquarium, next door (separate entry fee), is much the most interesting part. An attractive alternative is the Tierpark in Friedrichsfelde (U-Bahn line 6), although its subsidy is currently under threat.
Tierpark, Am Tierpark 125, Friedrichsfelde. Tel: 5100111. Open: daily 9am–dusk. U-Bahn to Tierpark.
Zoologischer Garten, Budapester Strasse 26. Tel: 254010. Open: daily 9am–6.30pm. U- or S-Bahn to Zoologischer Garten.

OTHER ATTRACTIONS

The circus regularly comes to town, as do fairgrounds. As these are movable feasts, it's best to consult *Berlin Programm* or *Tourist Information* for current details. Puppet theatres, while uniformly in German, are accessible enough, especially to the very young.
Grips
A favourite with German parents.
Altonaer Strasse 22. Tel: 3914004.

Sport

*B*erliners take their sport seriously. In fact the number of Berliners partici-
pating in sport is said to be on the increase, following a high profile campaign
by the local sports federation.

Sports facilities are well up to the mark
and most needs are catered for. Those
wishing to take gentle exercise will find
a surfeit of beautiful places in which to
go jogging, to walk or to take a swim.
As for spectator sports, ice hockey
remains a favourite here, while
basketball and American football are
beginning to catch on. Berlin is not,
however, renowned for its soccer, an
embarrassing shortcoming given
Germany's outstanding record in the
sport.

The best source of information for
visitors is *Berlin Programm*, its monthly
sporting calendar with full details of
addresses, telephones etc.

Another useful contact address is
Landessportbund Berlin, Jesse-Owens-
Allee 1–2. Tel: 300020.

The best overall sports facility is
Sport und Erholungszentrum (SEZ) at
Landsberger Allee 77, tel: 42283320,
where facilities include swimming pool,
fitness studio, skating rink, bowling
alley, volleyball and badminton courts.

BILLIARDS
Billiard Centrum
Popular with local enthusiasts.
Nollendorfplatz 3/4. Tel: 2163361.
U-Bahn to Nollendorfplatz.

BOATING
Rowing boats are available for hire on
any number of Berlin lakes – for
example, Freizeitpark Tegel,
Tiergarten (Neuer See) and Strandbad
Wannsee.

BOWLING
Bowling am Kurfürstendamm
The most central venue.
Kurfürstendamm 156. Tel: 8825030.
U-Bahn to Adenauer Platz.

CYCLING
The lack of hills makes Berlin a cyclist's
paradise. Bicycles can be rented from:
Fahrradbüro
*Hauptstrasse 146. Tel: 7845562. Closed:
Tuesday, Saturday and Sunday pm.*
U-Bahn to Kleistpark.
Also try Grunewald S-Bahn station
during the summer.
The most detailed map for cyclists is
ADFC-Radtourenkarte.

FISHING
For information on where to fish and
how to obtain the necessary licence,
contact:
Fischereiamt beim Senator für
Stadtentwicklung und
Umweltschutz
Havelchaussee 149. Tel: 3052047.

HORSE-RACING
Trabrennbahn Karlshorst
*Hermann-Duncker-Strasse 129 (trot
races).*
Galopprennbahn Hoppegarten
Goethetrasse 1 (gallop races).

ICE HOCKEY
Matches are held at the **Eissporthalle
Jafféstrasse**
*Tel: 30381. S-Bahn to Theodor-Heuss-
Platz.*

ICE-SKATING

There are rinks at the **Eissporthalle Jafféstrasse** (for details see **Ice Hockey** above); also at the **Eisstadion** *Fritz-Wildung-Strasse. Tel: 8234060. S-Bahn to Hohenzollern-Damm.*

RIDING

Berlin's main riding school is **Reitschule Onkel Toms Hütte** *Onkel-Tom-Strasse 172, Zehlendorf. Tel: 8132081.*

ROLLER SKATING

Roller Skating-Center
Hasenseide 108. Tel: 6211028.

RUNNING

The Berlin Marathon is held annually on the last Sunday in September or the first Sunday in October.

The Tiergarten is a popular venue for joggers.

SOCCER

Neither of Berlin's soccer teams is flourishing at the moment. For information on fixtures contact:
Berliner Fussball-Verband
Tel: 89111047.

SWIMMING

Indoor swimming at:
Blub
Buschkrugallee 64. Tel: 6066060.
There is also the Olympia-Schwimmstadion at Olympischer Platz. Outdoor swimming is available around many of the inland lakes and at Strandbad Wannsee, tel: 8035450.

TENNIS/SQUASH

Courts can be hired by the hour at
Tennis and Squash City
Brandenburgische Strasse 53. Tel: 879097.

Ice hockey is played at the Eissporthalle

Food and Drink

*I*n common with most of Central Europe, traditional German cuisine places the main emphasis on meat, especially pork, though the ubiquitous sausage is not *de rigeur*. Potatoes are the second chief ingredient, served up with pickled cabbage (*Sauerkraut*), beans, onions and peas. Gherkins have a habit of gate-crashing on virtually every meal. No one goes hungry in Germany – portions are huge and if by any chance you have room left for dessert, then the *Torten* and pastries represent a formidable challenge. Calorie-counting, needless to say, has no place in the traditional German kitchen.

Berlin cooking conforms largely to the German pattern. The local taste for salty food goes back to the time of Frederick the Great and the salt monopoly. Berliners were also traditionally great fans of the potato.

Local specialities include *Bouletten* (meat balls, introduced by the Huguenot community in the 17th century); *Aal grün* (eel served in a dill or parsley sauce), eel being in plentiful supply in the local rivers; and *Kartoffelpuffer* – the Berlin version of the savoury potato pancake. During the last 30 years,

however, there has been a revolution in the eating habits of the Berliner, thanks partly to the raising of health consciousness, but mainly to the influence of the immigrant communities from Yugoslavia, Italy, Turkey and the Middle East.

Nowadays young Berliners would rather opt for a pizza than a plateful of roast pork. 'New German Cuisine', which originated in the south, is also the rage, especially with the prosperous yuppie types. This places a firm emphasis on quality rather than quantity (many will find the portions mean) and on presentation. Standards are generally high but so are prices – too much so, in the opinion of many locals.

Tradition has been preserved in one respect, however: the Berliner still favours a large and varied breakfast, typically consisting of bread rolls and several kinds of sausage and eggs, and you'll find numerous cafés serving breakfast more or less throughout the day. This practice (theoretically) does away with the need for lunch and the increasing trend is for the main meal to be taken in the evening.

Which sausage? The choice in Berlin is overwhelming

If you haven't time for a sit-down meal, there are thousands of snack bars to choose from

TYPICAL DISHES AND SPECIALITIES

Soups and entrées
Hackepeter a kind of rissole
Kartoffelsuppe potato soup with bacon
Leberknödelsuppe dumpling soup with liver, onions, garlic
Linsensuppe lentil soup, often containing sausage
Soleier pickled eggs

Main courses
Berliner Schlachtplatte liver sausage, pig's kidneys and boiled pork
Eisbein pickled knuckle of pork, traditionally served with potatoes and *Sauerkraut*
Kartoffelpuffer a Berlin variant of fried potato cake
Kasseler Rippenspeer pickled pork chops, served with red cabbage – a Berlin speciality
Pellkartoffeln mit Quark jacket potatoes with curd cheese – and linseed oil if you want it!

Fish
Brathering grilled herring
Matjeshering raw herring fillets served with onion, apple and gherkins in cream

Dessert
Baumkuchen 'tree cake' made with potato flour, almonds and apricot jam.

Exotic drinks are on the menu at this downtown café

Sahara
Hawaii
Pylon-Flip
Ibiza
Bananenmilch
Managerdrink
Grüne Minna

Eating Out in Berlin

*I*n terms of sheer variety, Berlin, with its hundreds of restaurants offering every conceivable cuisine from around the world, is one of the best cities for eating out in the whole of Europe. Restaurants are concentrated on the west side, especially on the Ku'damm, in the streets off Savigny Platz and around Hardenbergstrasse, but you'll find them everywhere – so if you see a place that takes your fancy, note it down.

The best place for Turkish food is Kreuzberg, especially the streets near Kottbusser Tor and Schlesischer Tor stations. The east side of Berlin is slowly catching up with the west but still has a long way to go. The Nikolai Quarter (not cheap) and the Gendarmenmarkt are probably the safest bet here, or, if you're willing to travel a little, try Prenzlauer Berg (Schönhauser Allee and Husemannstrasse have a good selection of restaurants, many of them new).

Berlin is very much a late night city, so you can put off your meal while you rest and freshen up; however, many restaurants do tend to fill up quickly so if you're fussy be sure to make a reservation.

If you are keen to try traditional German food (which can, incidentally, be very good value) why not try a pub meal? Vegetarians are also well catered for in Berlin but it is advisable to use the specialist restaurants or those advertising international cuisine – picking from a German menu can be risky, as many dishes not specifying meat do in fact contain it hidden somewhere or other!

The variety of restaurants means that it is quite possible to eat cheaply – and if you're really short of money there's always the option of a kebab at any of the thousands of *imbiss* stands around the city. For a midday break, you can't beat the *Konditorei* or coffee and cake shop –

not cheap, but luxurious – regard it as a treat. Be aware when eating out that wine is quite expensive and tends to bump up the price of a meal in restaurants. Service and cover charges are generally included though it's customary to leave a tip with the waiter on payment (simply round up the price).

Inflation is still low in Germany but rising, so the following price guide can only be an indication. Many restaurants classed as expensive can work out much cheaper if you do without wine.

The following price guide is for an average meal per head, exclusive of drink:
D up to 15 DM
DD up to 30 DM
DDD up to 50 DM
DDDD up to 70 DM

GERMAN CUISINE
Altes Zollhaus DDDD
An attractive, secluded restaurant serving new German cuisine.
Carl-Herz-Ufer 30. Tel: 6923300. Open: Tuesday to Saturday 6–11pm. U-Bahn to Prinzenstrasse.
Ermelerhaus D/DDD
A splendid rococo mansion dating from 1703. Plain German fare downstairs, more exclusive meals in the Wein-restaurant upstairs.
Märkisches Ufer 10–12. Tel: 2793617 Open: daily 6pm–1am. U-Bahn to Märkisches Museum.

Dining out in front of the Kaiser Wilhelm Memorial Church

Friesenhof DD
This restaurant specialises in cooking from Friesland. Homely relaxed atmosphere.
Uhlandstrasse 185–6. Tel: 8836079. Open: daily 11.30am–midnight. U-Bahn to Uhlandstrasse.

Hardtke DD
Typical German food: Eisbein, Haxeu, Bockwurst etc.
Meinekestrasse 27. Tel: 8819827. Open: daily 10am–1am. U-Bahn to Kurfürstendamm.

Heinrich D
Reservations are advisable at this homely eating house. Excellent German cuisine.
Sophie-Charlotten-Strasse 88. Tel: 3216517. Open: daily noon–1am. U-Bahn to Oskar-Helene-Heim.

Storch DD
Boisterous, down-to-earth atmosphere with much talked-about Alsatian cuisine. Reservations essential.
Wartburgstrasse 54. Tel: 7842059. Open: daily 6pm–1am. Kitchen closes at 11.30pm. U-Bahn to Eisenacher Strasse.

THE BERLIN CAFÉ

It was an Austrian, Johann Georg Kranzler, who introduced the delights of the coffee shop to grateful Berliners in 1835. So successful was his venture that within 40 years the café scene was as vibrant here as in Vienna or Budapest. This was the golden age of the Berlin coffee house. By now, the Café Kranzler, on the corner of Friedrichstrasse, had taken over the first floor of its original premises and had introduced a smoking saloon and outdoor tables. Guests – customers would be too down-market for this establishment – were offered mouthwatering vol-au-vents in a mushroom and cream sauce, followed by a light gateau, served with the obligatory topping of *Schlagsahne* (whipped cream). The dishes were made from porcelain, bearing the hallmark of the KPM factory and the cutlery was handcrafted silver.

Just across the street from the Kranzler was the even more prestigious Café Bauer, a palatial establishment decorated with gilded mirrors, marble-topped tables, chandeliers and larger-than-life painted scenes from the lives of the Kaisers, attracting a clientele drawn almost exclusively from the aristocracy.

After World War I the focus of social life shifted towards the Ku'damm and the 'New West End'. The most famous establishment in this part of town was the Romanische Café, which once occupied the site of today's Europa- Center. Here one might encounter the novelist

The Café Kranzler and Café
Möhring are long-standing Berlin competitors

Thomas Mann, the famous opera star
Richard Tauber, or the latest film idol
hot out of the Babelsberg studios. Art
and culture, rather than high society,
was the meat of conversation here. If
you weren't familiar with Expressionism
or New Objectivity better find
somewhere else – perhaps the
Telschow where the pastry cook of the
same name delighted in his speciality,
the *Telschowschnitte*, a square pastry
packed with successive layers of hard
and soft chocolate with cream between
each.

Those days have long gone, but
the Berliner's love affair with the café
remains undiminished. The Café
Kranzler still exists, on the Ku'damm
rather than Unter den Linden and here,
or at the rival Café Möhring, visitors can
still choose from an enticing selection
of cakes and pastries: *Quark-
Kirschkuchen* (cheese cake with fresh
cherries), *Bienenstich* ('Bee-sting', with
its distinctive flavour of almonds and
butter icing), *Mokkatorte* (coffee
gateau), *Apfelkuchen* (apple cake),
Erdbeertorte (strawberry cake) – it
would be cruel to go on.

The traditional time to come is
about four in the afternoon, when
Berliners take tea with their friends.
There are the newspapers to read and
matters to discuss but, above all, the
coffee house is a place to daydream, to
off-load cares, and to slow down.

INTERNATIONAL CUISINE
Altes Luxemburg DDDD
This traditional restaurant is in great demand. The chef, Karl Wannemacher, recommends the guinea-fowl.
Reservations advisable.
Windscheidstrasse 31. Tel: 3238730. Open: Tuesday to Saturday 7–11pm. U-Bahn to Wilmersdorfer Strasse.

Borchardt DDD
The art nouveau décor is the main attraction.
Französische Strasse 47. Tel: 2293144. Open: daily 11.30am–2am. U-Bahn to Stadtmitte. Kitchen closes at midnight.

Lusiada DD
Lively and informal. The fish dishes are recommended.
Kurfürstendamm 132a. Tel: 8915869 Open: daily 5pm–4am. U-Bahn to Adenauer Platz.

Restauration 1900 DD
Smart café-restaurant in Prenzlauer Berg (on the corner of Kollwitz-Platz) with an excellent reputation.
Husemannstrasse 1. Tel: 4494052. Open: daily 4pm–12.30am. U-Bahn to Sennefelder Platz.

AMERICAN
Hard Rock Cafe, Berlin DD
Typical American cuisine.
Meinekestrasse 21. Tel: 884620. Open: daily noon–2am.

Lucky Strike Originals DD
A new venture specialising in Cajun food (Southern US) with specialities

Japanese sushi – one of many international dishes

like seafood gumbo.
Georgenstrasse 177/80. Tel: 30848822. Open: daily 10am–3am. U- or S–Bahn to Friedrichstrasse.

CHINESE
Ho Lin Wah DDD
A golden buddha presides over this restaurant in the former Chinese Embassy.
Kurfürstendamm 218. Tel: 8823271. Open: daily noon–midnight. U-Bahn Kurfürstendamm/Uhlandstrasse.

FRENCH
Reste Fidèle DD
Pleasant warm surroundings, attentive service, good food.
Bleibtreustrasse 41. Tel: 8811605. Open: 11am–2am. U-Bahn to Savignyplatz.

INDIAN
Kalkutta D
Boasts the only licensed clay oven in town to guarantee high quality tandoori dishes, so reserve a table if possible.
Bleibtreustrasse 17. Tel: 88366293. Open: daily noon–midnight. U-Bahn to Savignyplatz.

ITALIAN
Bar Centrale DD
A busy establishment with trendy clientele and excellent food.
Yorckstrasse 89. Tel: 7862989. Open: 6pm–3am. U-Bahn to Yorckstrasse.

Sugo D
Simple white décor, friendly atmosphere, reasonable prices.
Reichenberger Strasse

Kreuzberg is one of the places to go for Turkish cuisine

157. Tel: 6122303. Open: daily. U-Bahn
to Kottbusser Tor.

THAI
Tuk-Tuk DD
Comfortable atmosphere and authentic
Thai-Indonesian cooking.
*Grossgörschenstrasse 2. Tel: 7811588.
Open: daily 5.30pm–1am. U-Bahn to
Kleistpark.*

TURKISH
Bagdad D
A popular restaurant; the garden is
a plus.
*Schlesische Strasse 2. Tel: 6126962. Open:
daily. U-Bahn to Schlesisches Tor.*
Merhaba DD
Exotic and with a genuine Turkic
ambience; the food is reliable.
*Hasenheide 39. Tel: 6921713. Open:
Monday to Saturday 4pm–midnight.
U-Bahn to Südstern.*
Istanbul DD
Well-established, not cheap but the food
is authentic.
*Knesebeckstrasse 77. Tel: 8832777. Open:
daily noon–midnight. S-Bahn to
Savignyplatz.*

VEGETARIAN/FISH
Haquin DDD
Oriental and high quality; much talked
about.
*Martin-Luther-Strasse 1. Tel: 2182027.
Open: 6pm–11.30pm, except Thursday;
noon–3pm and 6–11.30pm weekends and
holidays. U-Bahn Wittenbergplatz.*

Turkish kebabs made to order at
Uhlandstrasse

Drink

*B*eer is the staple alcoholic drink in Berlin, much of it produced by the two large breweries: Schultheiss in Kreuzberg and Berliner Kindl. Other German beers, as well as foreign varieties, are also in plentiful supply in pubs, especially in the trendier *Szene* (hang-outs) around Savignyplatz or out in Kreuzberg and Prenzlauer Berg.

Ask for *ein Bier* or *ein Pils* and you'll usually be presented with a glass of light draught beer (to be certain, ask for *Bier vom Fass*). If you want a bottle, ask for *eine Flasche*. In summer, *Berliner Weisse mit Schuss* appears on the menu. This is a low-alcohol beer sweetened with a dash of raspberry juice or *mit grün*, extract of green woodruff. Sometimes the waiter or waitress will bring the drink to your table when it has settled, but there's no hard and fast rule. Bars stay open all day and (except in the Mitte) well into the night – until three or four in the morning in some places (Nollendorfplatz, for example) – though 1am is more common. Generally, pubs and cafés are extremely welcoming places though the service in some Kreuzberg pubs can be a bit sullen – take this with a pinch of salt: it's a pose.

Although Germany is famous as a wine-producing country, Berlin is not a wine-producing region. Most of the pubs in the centre of town double up as wine bars and, both here and in restaurants, there is a wide range of German and international wines. Popular German varieties include *Riesling* and *Sekt* (sparkling wine). If you want a dry wine ask for *Trocken*; the word for sweet is *süss*. For those who don't like or don't want to drink alcohol, *ein Mineralwasser* will bring you a bottle of mineral water, usually carbonated. If you want it plain, say *ohne Kohlensäure*.

BARS AND CAFÉS
Café Bleibtreu
Sophisticated atmosphere, popular with the young set.
Bleibtreustrasse 45. Open: 9.30am–1am, Friday and Saturday to 2.30am. U-Bahn Savignyplatz.

Café Kranzler
Berlin's most famous coffee house, with a tradition going back to the 19th century. Terrace overlooking Ku'damm. *Kurfürstendamm 18. Tel: 8826911. Open: 8am–midnight. U-Bahn to Kurfürstendamm.*

Brewing is an art long-familiar to Berlin

Cafe Möhring
Old-fashioned coffee house where the waitresses wear starched white aprons.
Kurfürstendamm 213. Tel: 8812075. Open: 7am–midnight. U-Bahn to Uhlandstrasse.

Dicke Wirtin
The 'Fat Lady' is a traditional Berlin *kneipe* (see pages 172–3) popular with students.
Carmerstrasse 9. Open: noon until late. U- or S-Bahn to Zoologischer Garten.

Eisenwerk
Typical *Szene* in Prenzlauer Berg.
Sredzkistrasse 33. Open: from 6pm until late. U-Bahn to Eberswalder Strasse.

Elefant
Lively, atmospheric bar typical of the Kreuzberg scene.
Heinrichplatz. Open: 8pm until late. U-Bahn to Hermannplatz.

Harry's New York Bar
Piano bar in the Hotel Esplanade, attracting a mainly business clientele.
Lützowufer 15. Tel: 261011. Open: noon–3am. U-Bahn to Nollendorfplatz.

Leydicke
Dating from 1877, this is one of the oldest *kneipen* in Berlin. Justly famous.
Mansteinstrasse 4. Tel: 2162973. Open: Monday, Tuesday, Thursday and Friday 4pm–midnight; Wednesday, Saturday and Sunday 11am–1am. U-Bahn to Yorckstrasse.

Berliner Weisse (beer and crème de menthe) – a tipple for the sweet-toothed

Rote Harfe
On the same square as the Elefant (see above) and equally congenial.
Heinrichplatz. Open: 8am until late. U-Bahn to Hermannplatz.

Schwarzes Café
Long opening hours make this a popular haunt of night-clubbers.
Kantstrasse 148. Tel: 3138038. Open: 5pm–5am. S-Bahn to Savignyplatz.

Wilhelm Hoeck
Friendly, lively atmosphere.
Wilmersdorfer Strasse 149. Open: 8am–midnight. U-Bahn to Adenauerplatz.

Zum Nussbaum
Warm and cosy but small, so liable to get crowded. Originally 16th-century, the 'Nut Tree' is in the Nikolaiviertel (Nikolai Quarter).
Propstrasse. Tel: 24313328. Open: noon–2am. U-Bahn to Alexanderplatz.

Berlin pubs guarantee visitors a warm welcome

Every Berliner has his favourite pub – The Fat Lady, Beer Heaven, The Sturdy Dog, The Last Resort, Pig's Trotter Corner; for the inhabitants of this beer-loving and convivial city, the *Kneipe* is a home-from-home, a living room and a meeting point, a centre for gossip and diversion, a forum for discussion and for putting the world to rights. And there are plenty of pubs to choose from – more than 4,000 at the last count. But the traditional Berlin *Kneipe* is becoming something of an endangered species, especially in the more salubrious parts of the city. Dark forces are at work here in the insidious guise of changing tastes. Look for the tell-tale signs: brightly painted walls,

smart chromium counters, no-smoking signs, foreign beers and – most pernicious of all – loud rock music.

Despite this worrying trend, the honest to goodness *Eck-Kneipe* (corner pub) can still be found in the old working class neighbourhoods of Kreuzberg, Prenzlauer Berg and the Mitte. They can be identified by the brewery logo over the entrance (Berliner Kindl, Schultheiss), by the yellowing net curtains, the contented expression on the faces of the clientele and the ubiquitous billiard table. Heavy drinking, let's be honest, is not uncommon here, alcoholism not unknown. But gone are the days, more than a century ago, when the Social

THE BERLIN *KNEIPE*

Democratic Party had to appeal to its working class members to 'abstain from alcohol' and turn instead to more dignified leisure pursuits. As the density of pubs in Berlin at that time was more than twice that of comparable industrial cities in Europe it is perhaps not surprising that the appeal fell largely on deaf ears.

Today, as in the past, the *Kneipe* is a place of die-hard custom and time-honoured tradition. Woe betide the drinker (ignorance can be no excuse) who ignores an invitation to clink glasses or the visitor who inadvertently occupies the *Stammtisch*, the table reserved for regulars. Canny tipplers melt into the crowd by ordering a *Korn* (a light beer with a schnapps chaser) or a measure of the caraway seed liqueur called *Kümmel*.

Every *Kneipe* worth its salt serves the traditional local delicacies: roll mop (pickled herring), *solei* (pickled eggs), *Aal grün* (eel served in a dill or parsley sauce) and *Hackepeter* (a kind of meatloaf) – plain, no-nonsense fare.

Finally, a word of advice: visting a *Kneipe* can be addictive – you have been warned!

The *Kneipe* is a home from home for the traditionally-minded Berliner

Hotels and Accommodation

*T*here is no shortage of accommodation in Berlin – from luxury hotels to hotel-pensions and youth hostels – and the situation can only get better at the end of the current building boom. Furthermore, a surprisingly large number of hotels of every category are situated right in the heart of the city – no more than a few minutes' walk from the Ku'damm.

Most visitors to Berlin still prefer to stay in the western half. The east side suffers from a surfeit of hotels in the top price category, a hangover from the days when the government was anxious to relieve western travellers of their hard currency. Expect the situation to improve dramatically over the next 10 years. Standards of service, notoriously poor under the old regime, are also gradually improving, although there are still pockets of resistance.

The Bristol Hotel Kempinski has a famous reputation to live up to

PRICES

Generally speaking, hotel prices are much the same as in other European capitals. At the top end of the market the sky is the limit, although guests generally get what they pay for. The star ratings of former East Berlin hotels, however, should be taken with a pinch of salt – standards vary. The greatest variation is in hotels of the middle category.

Where Berlin scores highest is in the range and quantity of cheap accommodation. There are thousands of pensions, and not all are outside the central districts. Even if they are, remember that the public transport system is excellent.

The following is an indication of what one might expect to pay for a double room in a Berlin hotel. Needless to say, inflation is bound to push prices up, although competition should prevent dramatic increases. Breakfast is generally included in the price of accommodation, but it's best to check.
5 star 400DM or above
4 star 300–400DM
3 star 200–300DM
2 star 150–200DM
1 star up to 150DM

LOCATION

The greatest concentration of hotel accommodation of all types is around the Ku'damm and the more accessible parts of Charlottenburg. There are a

Rooms with a view over the Spree – the Palasthotel on Karl-Liebknecht Strasse

number of large hotels in the Mitte district, almost uniformally expensive. Anyone wishing to stay in the historic heart of the city should bear in mind that the east side still offers very little in the way of nightlife, although some hotels do have high-quality restaurants. A great deal of lower price accommodation is clustered in two central western districts, Schöneberg and Kreuzberg – Kreuzberg, in particular, will appeal to younger people. There is plenty of scope for anyone wishing to stay outside the city – in Wannsee, for example, or Grunewald – and not all the hotels here are expensive. Eastern beauty spots like Müggelsee or Köpenick may work out cheaper but are generally more remote.

BOOKING

Unless there is a sudden influx of visitors on the scale of 1989–90, it should not be essential to book in advance. However, to get the hotel of your choice, it is advisable to plan ahead. Also bear in mind that demand increases dramatically at certain times of the year – during the Berlin Film Festival, for example (towards the end of February), as well as throughout July and August. Many top hotels increase their rates when there are conferences on, so check carefully. For last minute booking, see the agencies on page 176, but remember that hotels claiming to be full do sometimes have rooms available when pressed. Most hotels and pensions require a deposit in advance and some even insist on payment in full within a day or two of arrival.

Travellers who purchase their tickets from a Thomas Cook network location are entitled to use the services of any other Thomas Cook location free of charge to make hotel reservations.

Berlin's largest hotel is the Intercontinental, with rooms overlooking the Kaiser Wilhelm Memorial Church

BOOKING AGENCIES IN BERLIN
First Hotel Reservierung
This agency charges no fee and will book you into one of a number of quality hotels, including the Savoy, at short notice.
Landgrafenstrasse 3. Tel: 8811515.

Mitwohnzentrale
These agencies find private rooms and apartments for longer-stay guests, starting from one week. The best is at:
3rd floor, Ku'damm-Eck, Kurfürstendamm 227/8. Tel: 8826694.

Reservierungsdienst Berlin
An agency which has 8,000 beds on its books and which also leases apartments.
Tel: 8221879.

Verkehrsamt Berlin
Tourist information will ring around for you and charge only a small fee.
Europa-Center. Tel: 2626031.

For short-stay private accommodation, enquire at the Tourist Information Office on Budapester Strasse.

HOTELS
Luxury hotels
Berlin has a number of top-class hotels with facilities to match. One of the

newest is the Grand Hotel Esplanade
(tel: 261011), beautifully designed and
not far from the Tiergarten. This is not
to be confused with the Grand-Hotel
(tel: 23270) on Friedrichstrasse, another
modern hotel occupying a prime site just
off Unter den Linden and trying to
recapture the traditions of the past.
Berlin's largest hotel, with rooms
overlooking the Kaiser-Wilhelm
Memorial Church, is the Inter-
Continental (tel: 26020). It has several
top-class restaurants, including Zum
Hugenotten and the roof-top
Dachgarten.

Traditional hotels

Unfortunately, none of Berlin's
magnificent pre-war hotels has survived.
However, there are a number of modern
establishments anxious to recapture past
glories. Leading the field is the Bristol
Kempinski (tel: 883340), on the
Ku'damm, descendant of the famous
hotel that used to look out on Unter den
Linden. The Savoy (tel: 311030) is
another hotel with a famous name to live
up to. The Kronprinz (tel: 896030) is at
the western end of the Ku'damm, and
anyone wishing to sample the flavour of
the 19th-century Mitte at a moderate
price might like to stay in the
Charlottenhof (tel: 238060), right
opposite the Gendarmenmarkt.
Riehmers Hofgarten is a beautiful
late19th-century mansion which is
situated in an attractive part of
Kreuzberg.

Out of town

There is a large choice of hotels of all
types situated in the leafy suburbs or out
among the lakes and woods. The
Forsthaus Paulsborn (tel: 8138010) is a
sedate period hotel and restaurant

situated deep in the Grunewald forest.
The Belvedere (tel: 8260010) offers the
best of both worlds – a location close
to Grunewald yet not far from
Charlottenburg and the Ku'damm.
Wannseeblick (tel: 8100070), as the
name suggests, has fine views across the
lake, while the Sorat Humboldt-Mühle
(tel: 439040) occupies a converted
industrial mill in Tegel which backs
directly on to the water.

Pensions/budget hotels

There are literally hundreds of these and
by no means all are banished to the
outer reaches of town. However, match
phone numbers with addresses before
you book. Pension Kreuzberg (tel:
2513064) is a favourite with students
while both the Econtel Berlin (tel:
34681147), near Schloss Charlottenburg
and Hotel-Pension Wittelsbach (tel:
876345 – U-Bahn to Konstanzer
Strasse) cater for children. The
Artemisia Hotel (tel: 878905) is for
women only and is excellent value for
money and centrally situated.

Youth hostels

There are a number in Berlin. Bear in
mind that if you stay out of town the
curfew will preclude joining in the night
life; also that the hostels in the best
locations are in great demand during
summer. The most central of all is the
Jugendgästenhaus am Zoo (tel:
3921410); next comes the
Jugendgästhaus on Kluckstrasse (tel:
2611097), not far from the Tiergarten.
More remote are the Jugendherberge
Wannsee (tel: 8032034) and
Jugendherberge Ernst Reuter (tel:
4041610). You'll need an International
Youth Hostel Federation card for most
youth hostels.

On Business

*B*erlin's peculiar political status before 1989 practically disqualified it as a centre for international business. Today the situation is changing fast – investment levels in Berlin are unprecedented and the prospects can only get better when the German government finally moves here in 2000. Major international firms like Sony are already looking for rich pickings and lucrative contracts. The city government is particularly anxious to establish a reputation for Berlin as a centre for international conferences.

BUSINESS HOURS

Most businesses and government offices are open 9am–6pm Monday to Friday, though some open Saturday 9am–2pm. Banking hours are 9am–3pm Monday to Friday, though some banks close at 1pm. Most banks have extended hours on one or two days a week.

CHARTERED FLIGHTS
Windrose Air

Flies private chartered flights to Berlin Tempelhof from destinations all over Europe. Also hotel reservations, rented cars, theatre tickets and restaurant reservations.

Airport Tempelhof, 12101 Berlin. Tel: 6952400/12, fax: 6951404.

CONFERENCE CENTRES AND TRADE FAIRS
Hotel Steigenberger Berlin

An attractive modern hotel, centrally located. Siemens portable computers and software are available to guests on request. *Los-Angeles-Platz 1. Tel: 21270, fax: 2127117. U-Bahn to Kurfürstendamm.*

Internationales Congress Centrum

This enormous space-age complex on the

No better place to do business in – the National Congress Centre

western fringes of the city opened in 1979. Facilities include 80 conference and meeting rooms, banqueting halls, banks, shops and restaurants.
Messedamm 22. Tel: 30380. Open: Monday to Friday noon–6pm, Saturday 10am–2pm. U-Bahn to Kaiserdamm.

Inter-Continental Hotel Business Centre
A favourite base for German and international business men and women, the centre is equipped with Philips' personal computers, laser printers, desktop publishing facilities, photocopiers and portable telephones. One much appreciated feature is the secretarial service. An interpreter service is also available. There are a number of executive suites in the centre, each provided with its own telephone number, outside line and fax. The hotel can accommodate up to 1,250 conference participants. There is a bus direct to and from the airport.
Budapester Strasse 2. Tel: 26020, fax: 260280760. U-Bahn to Wittenbergplatz.

Keeping abreast of events at the Intercontinental Business Centre

Mondial Hotel
The hotel's ideal location on the Kurfürstendamm and its relaxed atmosphere are its main recommendations. Conference facilities.
Kurfürstendamm 47. Tel: 884110, fax: 88411150. U-Bahn to Uhlandstrasse.

COURIERS
DHL
Overnight courier, international service.
Kaiserin-Augusta-Allee 16–24. Tel: 3478511. Last pick-up in city area 4pm. Letters and packages up to 6pm.

GERMAN LANGUAGE
Berlin International Language School
Offers a special course in business German.
Nassauische Strasse 57. Tel: 878279.

OFFICE STATIONERY
Wolff & Matthes
Ritterstrasse 12–14. Tel: 6146088, fax: 6146020.

OTHER SERVICES
Berolina Berlin-Service
Helps with the planning of conferences and conventions, makes hotel reservations, provides guide services, organises transfers and special tours.
Meinekestrasse 3. Tel: 8822091, fax: 8824128.

Bus-Verkehr-Berlin KG (BVB)
Organises sight-seeing tours and programmes and coach rentals, makes hotel reservations and arranges trade fair programmes.
Kurfürstendamm 225. Tel: 8859880, fax: 8813508.

Practical Guide

CONTENTS

Tegel. There is a frequent bus and taxi service from the airport to the city centre. U-Bahn to Bahnhof Zoologischer Garten or Bus 109 to Budapester Strasse.

The old military airport at Tempelhof handles a limited number of charter as well as domestic flights. There are no exchange facilities at this airport but it is the closest to the city centre. U-Bahn line 6 to Friedrichstrasse.

The third international airport, Berlin Schönefeld, is on the east side of the city and still deals mainly in flights from Russia and eastern Europe. Increasingly, however, charter companies are making use of this airport.

There is a regular coach service into town; or S-Bahn lines 9 and 10 to the Friedrichstrasse. An Airport-Transfer bus runs between Tegel and Schönefeld.

By rail

There are international train connections to Berlin from Paris, Brussels, Copenhagen, Warsaw, Moscow, Vienna, and Prague. The *Thomas Cook European Timetable*, which is published monthly and gives up-to-date details of most rail services and many shipping services throughout Europe, will help you plan a rail journey to, from and around Germany. It is available in the UK from some stations, any branch of Thomas Cook or by phoning 01733 268943. In the USA, contact the Forsyth Travel Library Inc, 9154 West 57th St (PO Box 2975), Shawnee Mission, Kansas 66201; tel: (800) 367 7982 (toll-free).

German National Tourist Offices

UK 65 Curzon Street, London W1Y 7PE. Tel: 0171 495 3990.

ARRIVING
By air

There are three airports in Berlin. Most regular and chartered flights depart from

US 747 3rd Avenue, 33rd floor, New York 10017. Tel: 212 308 3300.

Entry formalities

A valid passport or national identity card is required by EC nationals. A valid passport is required by Australian, Canadian, US and New Zealand passport holders; all other nationals will need a visa.

Travellers who require visas should obtain them in their country of residence, as it may prove difficult to obtain them elsewhere. In the UK, the Thomas Cook Passport and Visa Service can advise on and obtain the necessary documentation – consult your Thomas Cook travel representative.

BABYSITTERS

Heinnzelmännchen Unter den Eichen 96. Tel: 8316071.
TUSMA Hardenbergstrasse 35. Tel: 3134054.

BICYCLES

Berlin is well provided with cycle lanes. Bicycles may be taken on the S- or U-Bahn: board at the doors with the relevant sign. You will need an *Ermässigungstarif* (reduced rate ticket). Bicycles can be hired at:
Fahrradbüro Hauptstrasse 146. Tel: 7845562.
Berlin By Bike Möckenstrasse 92. Tel: 2169177.

BERLIN THROUGH THE YEAR

February – Berlin International Film Festival.
March – International Tourism Exchange.
May – The Peace Race: cyclists from all over eastern Europe.
10 May – Writers gather in Bebelplatz to commemorate the 1933 book-burning.
July – Jazz in July Festival.
September – Berlin Arts Festival.
October – Berlin Marathon (first Sunday) and the Berlin Motor Show.
3 October – German Unity Day.
October, November – Jazz-fest Berlin.
9 November – Anniversary of Wall opening.
31 December – New Year celebrations at Brandenburg Gate.

CAMPING

Deutschen Camping-Clubs eV
Geisbergstrasse 11, Berlin. Tel: 246071. This organisation runs three campsites on the outskirts of town which are clean, well-run and cheap.

CHURCHES AND OTHER PLACES OF WORSHIP

Anglican St George's, Pleussenallee. Holy Communion – Sunday 8am. Morning Service – 10am.
Catholic St Hedwig's Cathedral, Bebelplatz. Four masses on Sunday: 8am, 10am, 11.30am, 6pm. Tel: 2004761.
Islamic There are a number of mosques in Kreuzberg – contact Tourist Information for service times.
Jewish Conservative: Synagogue Pestalozzistrasse 14. Tel: 3138411. Services Friday 6pm, Saturday 9.30am; and Orthodox: Adass Jisroel, Tucholsky Strasse 40. Services Friday 5pm, Saturday 9.30am. Or contact Jüdisches Gemeindehaus in Fasanenstrasse 79–80. Tel: 88842030.
Protestant Kaiser-Wilhelm-Gedächtnis-Kirche, Breitscheidplatz. Tel: 2185023. Sunday services 10am and 6pm. There is a service in English at 9am during the summer.

CLIMATE
See page 14.

CONVERSION TABLES
See tables opposite.

CRIME
Generally Berlin is a safe city but visitors should take the usual precautions against thieves. Leave large amounts of money in the hotel safe, carry a money belt, take extra care in crowds and on the underground. While travelling at night be aware that lighting is poor on the east side of the city. Make sure to report thefts and other crimes promptly to the police for insurance purposes.

CRISIS LINE
In case of rape, contact the rape crisis line on Stresemanstrasse 40. Tel: 2512828.

DISABLED TRAVELLERS
Buses have rear-door access and safety straps for wheelchairs. For help with renting wheelchairs and other problems or for information contact:
Deutscher Paritätischer Wohlfahrtsverband, Brandenburgischestrasse 80. Tel: 860010; or **Landesamt für Zentral Soziale Aufgaben,** Landes-versorgungsamt, Sächsischestrasse 28–30. Tel: 8676114.

DRIVING
A driving licence, national identity plate and vehicle registration certificate are required. Germans drive on the right. Speed limits are 130kmph (81mph) on motorways; 100kmph (62mph) on major roads; 50 kmph (31mph) in built-up areas. Fines for traffic offences are payable on the spot and police are empowered to remove car keys. It is illegal to drive after consuming alcohol and penalties are stiff.

Car rental
Hertz and other major firms operate from Tegel airport and major hotels.

EMBASSIES AND CONSULATES
Australia Kempinski Plaza, Uhlandstrasse 181/3 Berlin. Tel: 8800880.
Canada IHZ Building, Friedrichstrasse 95 10117 Berlin. Tel: 2611161.
UK Unter den Linden 32/4 10117 Berlin. Tel: 201840.
US Neustädtischer Kirchstrasse 4/5 10017 Berlin. Tel: 2385174.

EMERGENCY TELEPHONE NUMBERS
Police 110
Fire and **ambulance** 112
Doctor (24-hour) tel: 310031
Dentist (24-hour) tel: 1141.

WEATHER CONVERSION CHART
25.4mm = 1 inch
°F = 1.8 × °C + 32

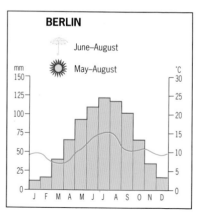

BERLIN

June–August
May–August

Men's Suits

UK		36	38	40	42	44	46	48
Rest of Europe		46	48	50	52	54	56	58
US		36	38	40	42	44	46	48

Dress Sizes

UK		8	10	12	14	16	18
France		36	38	40	42	44	46
Italy		38	40	42	44	46	48
Rest of Europe		34	36	38	40	42	44
US		6	8	10	12	14	16

Men's Shirts

UK	14	14.5		15	15.5	16	16.5	17
Rest of Europe	36	37		38	39/40	41	42	43
US	14	14.5		15	15.5	16	16.5	17

Men's Shoes

UK	7	7.5	8.5		9.5	10.5	11
Rest of Europe	41	42	43		44	45	46
US	8	8.5	9.5		10.5	11.5	12

Women's Shoes

UK		4.5	5	5.5	6	6.5	7
Rest of Europe	38	38	39	39		40	41
US		6	6.5	7	7.5	8	8.5

Conversion Table

FROM	TO	MULTIPLY BY
Inches	Centimetres	2.54
Feet	Metres	0.3048
Yards	Metres	0.9144
Miles	Kilometres	1.6090
Acres	Hectares	0.4047
Gallons	Litres	4.5460
Ounces	Grams	28.35
Pounds	Grams	453.6
Pounds	Kilograms	0.4536
Tons	Tonnes	1.0160

To convert back, for example from
centimetres to inches, divide by the number
in the the third column.

HEALTH AND INSURANCE

Up-to-date health advice can be
obtained from your Thomas Cook travel
consultant or direct from Thomas Cook
Travel Clinic, 45 Berkeley Street,
London, WlA 1EB, tel: 0171 408 4157.
This is open for consultation without
appointment Monday to Friday
8.30am–5.30pm and can give
vaccinations and medical advice.

There are no mandatory vaccination
requirements and no vaccination
recommendations other than to keep
tetanus and polio immunisation up to
date. Like every other part of the world,
AIDS is present. AIDS helpline:
Berliner AIDS-Hilfe eV, Meinekestrasse
12, tel: 8833017.

All EC countries have reciprocal
arrangements for reclaiming the costs of
medical services. UK residents should
obtain forms CM1 and E111 from any
post office in the UK. This provides
detailed information as to how to claim
and what is covered. Claiming is often a
laborious and long drawn-out process
and you are only covered for medical
care, not for emergency repatriation,
holiday cancellation and so on. You are
therefore strongly advised to take out a
travel insurance policy.

HOLIDAYS

1 January
Good Friday
Easter Monday
1 May
Ascension Day
Whit Monday
3 October – German Unity Day
1 November – All Saints Day
November – (movable date) Buss-und-
  Bettag, Day of Repentance and Prayer
Christmas Day
26 December.

LANGUAGE

Knowledge of English is increasingly common in Berlin but efforts to speak German will be appreciated.

Words/phrases

yes	*ja*
no	*nein*
please	*bitte*
thank you	*danke*
good morning	*guten Morgen*
good evening	*guten Abend*
good night	*gute Nacht*
small	*klein*
large	*gross*
quickly	*schnell*
cold	*kalt*
hot	*warm*
good	*gut*
room	*Zimmer*
menu	*Speisekarte*
breakfast	*Frühstück*
en lunch	*Mittagessen*
dinner	*Abendessen*
white wine	*Weisswein*
red wine	*Rotwein*
bread	*Brot*
milk	*Milch*
water	*Wasser*
on the right	*rechts*
on the left	*links*
straight on	*geradeaus*
open	*offen*
closed	*geschlossen*
near	*nahe*
far	*weit*
how much	*wieviel*
expensive	*teuer*
cheap	*billig*
excuse me please	*entschuldigen Sie bitte*
do you speak English?	*sprechen Sie Englisch?*

Days of the week

Monday	*Montag*
Tuesday	*Dienstag*
Wednesday	*Mittwoch*
Thursday	*Donnerstag*
Friday	*Freitag*
Saturday	*Sonnabend*
Sunday	*Sonntag*

Numbers

one	*eins*
two	*zwei*
three	*drei*
four	*vier*
five	*fünf*
six	*sechs*
seven	*sieben*
eight	*acht*
nine	*neun*
ten	*zehn*

LIBRARY
British Council Library,
Hardenbergstrasse 20. Tel: 310716.
Open: Monday to Friday noon–6pm.
English books.

LOST PROPERTY
Fundbüro der Polizei, Platz der
Luftbrücke 6. Tel: 6990.
BVG (public transport), Lorenzweg 5.
Tel: 7518021. Open: Monday, Tuesday
and Thursday 9am–3pm; Wednesday
9am–6pm; Friday 9am–2pm.

MEDIA
Newspapers
There are several Berlin dailies:
Tagesspiegel and *Berliner Morgenpost* are
the main ones. Foreign-language
newspapers are sold in stands and shops
around Zoo station and the Ku'damm
and are also available in some cafés.
Internationale Presse Kiosk,
Hardenbergstrasse. Tel: 8817256.
Open: daily from 8am–midnight, selling
a variety of newspapers and periodicals.
Radio
BBC World service – 90.2 FM.
Forces radios still exist on (British)
BFBC 98.8FM and (American) AFN
87.9FM.

MONEY
The unit of currency in Germany is the
Deutsche Mark. One DM equals 100
pfennigs.
Exchange offices
AGW Joachimsthaler Strasse, 1–3
(open: Monday to Friday 8am–8pm,
Saturday 9am–3pm).
Wechselstuben offering acceptable
exchange rates can be found everywhere
in Berlin. Friedrichstrasse Station is
open 24 hours a day.
　　Major credit cards: American

Express, Diners Club, MasterCard,
Visa, EuroCard and JCB are
acceptable but cards are used less
readily than in some other countries,
so check first. American Express:
Friedrichstrasse 172, tel: 2384102;
Uhlandstrasse 173/4, tel: 8827575.
　　Thomas Cook MasterCard
travellers' cheques free you from the
hazards of carrying large amounts of
cash and in the event of loss or theft
can quickly be refunded. Emergency
telephone number: 0130–85–99–30
(toll-free 24-hour).
　　Deutsche Mark cheques are
recommended, though cheques
denominated in US dollars and other
European currencies are accepted.
Hotel shops and some restaurants
accept some travellers' cheques in lieu
of cash.
　　The following Network Members of
Thomas Cook can provide emergency
assistance in the case of loss and theft
of Thomas Cook MasterCard
travellers' cheques. The Thomas Cook
Foreign Exchange branches (marked
'FE') also provide full foreign
exchange facilities.

Thomas Cook ReiseCentre,
Bayreuther Strasse 37 (FE)
Thomas Cook ReiseCentre,
Friedrichstrasse 56 (FE).
Thomas Cook Reisebüro,
Breitestrasse 39, Berlin-Pankow (FE).
Thomas Cook Reisebüro, Helios
GmbH, Uhlandstrasse 73.

OPENING TIMES
Pharmacies (*Apotheke*) have late
opening times posted in the window or
tel: 310031 for information.
Europa-Apotheke Tauentzienstrasse 9.
Tel: 2614142. Open: daily 9am–9pm.

Trams are still a common sight on the eastern side of town

Banks

Open: Monday to Friday
8.15am–12.30pm; afternoon opening
times vary.
Berliner Bank at Tegel Airport is open
from 8am–10pm.

Shops

See pages 142–5.

PERSONAL SAFETY

Berlin is a non-violent city by and large,
but visitors might do well to avoid the
red light district around Potsdamer
Strasse late at night. Employees of the
U-bahn will call a taxi for women
travelling alone after 8pm.

PHOTOPROCESSING

Photo Huber (one-hour processing)
Europa-Center. Tel: 2624666.

POST OFFICES

Bahnhof Zoo (24-hour). Tel: 3139799.
Hauptbahnhof, Strasse der Pariser
Kommune 8–12. Tel: 5800871. Open:
8am–9pm.

Local post offices – open: Monday to
Friday 8am–6pm, Saturday, 8am–noon.
Post boxes are bright yellow. Stamp
machines can be found in central areas
and outside post offices.

PUBLIC TRANSPORT

See pages 24–5.
For information about all public
transport in the Berlin area: BVG-

U-BAHN AND S-BAHN

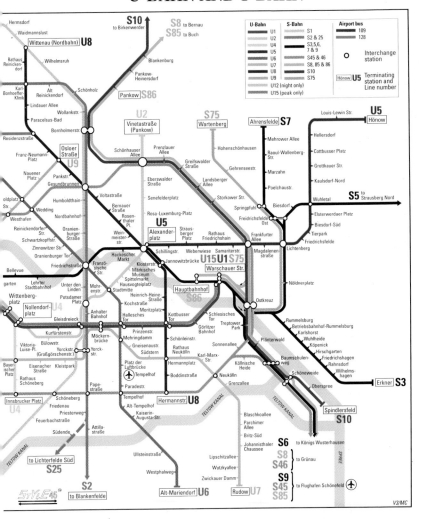

Pavillon, Hardenbergplatz, (Bahnhof Zoo). Tel: 2562462. Open: Monday to Friday 8am–6pm, Saturday 7am–2pm, Sunday 9am–4pm.

Train information – German National Railway (Bundesbahn), Hardenbergstrasse 20. Tel: 19419. Open: Monday to Friday 8.30am–6.30pm.

SENIOR CITIZENS

On presentation of an identity card senior citizens are entitled to half-price admission to museums and reductions on public transport, river boat tickets, etc.

STUDENT AND YOUTH TRAVEL

An International Student Identity Card (ISIC) entitles the holder to discounts at museums and some theatres of up to 50 per cent. The publication *Berlin For Young People* is available from Tourist Information. Youth hostels – see page 177.

Watch this space! Keeping up to date with events in Berlin is a full-time occupation

Ticket machine, Friedrichstrasse S-Bahn

TAXIS

Tel: 6902 or 2610. For chauffeur service tel: 2139090.

TELEPHONES

Many public phone boxes are marked *Kartentelefon* and are operated by phonecards (sold at post offices). Booths marked *International* or telephones in post offices are for long-distance calls. The code for Berlin from abroad is 030
Operator 03
International operator 0010
Directory enquiries 01188
International enquiries 00118
Telegrams 1131.

TIME

Berlin is one hour ahead of GMT in the winter and two hours ahead in the summer.

TIPPING

Service charges are included in prices so tipping is unnecessary, but customary by rounding off the bill.

TOILETS

Most public toilets are free. Men – *Herren*; Women – *Damen* or *Frauen*.

TOURIST INFORMATION

Berlin Touristik Information, Martin-Luther-Strasse 105. Tel: 21234. Open: Monday to Friday 8am–7pm; Saturday 8am–4pm.

Verkehrsamt Berlin, Europa-Center. Tel: 2626031. Open: daily 8am–4pm. Hotel bookings 8am–10.30pm.

Bahnhof Zoo. Tel: 3139063. Open: daily 8am–11pm.

Tegel airport. Tel: 41013145. Open: daily 8am–11pm.

Tourist Information is about to be privatised and amalgamated with hotel reservations.

Phoning home couldn't be easier in Berlin

ACKNOWLEDGEMENTS

The Automobile Association wishes to thank the following organisations, libraries and photographers for their assistance in the preparation of this book.

BERLIN TOURIST BOARD 161, 173b; **MARY EVANS PICTURE LIBRARY** 130; **GALERIE PELS-LEUSDEN** 157; **NATURE PHOTOGRAPHERS LTD** 140a, 140b, (P R Sterry); **LUDWIG SCHIRMER** 67; **SPECTRUM COLOUR LIBRARY** 10, 11a; **THE RONALD GRANT ARCHIVE** 146/7, 147, 152a, 152/3, 153; **ZEFA PICTURE LIBRARY (UK) LTD** cover, inset, spine.

The remaining photographs are held in the AA Photo Library and were taken by Antony Souter with the exception of pages 11b, 15, 16, 17a, 18, 37, 47, 61, 66, 68, 75, 84, 86, 88, 89, 99, 150, 165, 166, 167, 174 and 175 which were taken by Adrian Baker and pages 126, 127, 128, 129, 141 and 173a which were taken by Doug Traverso.

CONTRIBUTORS
Series Adviser: Melissa Shales   **Designer:** Design 23   **Copy Editor:** Nia Williams
Verifier: Adi Kraus   **Indexer:** Marie Lorimer